Men, Women & Children Touched by War

By
Harold E. Davis

Men, Women & Children Touched by War

No part of this book shall be used or reproduced in any manner whatsoever without written permission. For information, contact Harold E. Davis, 8740 W. 69th Street, Shawnee Mission, KS 66204. E-mail: seagull31@gmail.com

Library of Congress Control Number: 2008911846

ISBN: 1-4392-2739-X

Published by:
BookSurge, a division
of Amazon.com
2009

Other books by Harold E. Davis: *I Survived Ploesti, The Story of Ralph Ray Guillinger, Combat Navigator of WWII* and *The Heart and Soul of America, Experiences and Antics of WWII Flyers.*

FOREWORD

Throughout our nation's history, there are extraordinary stories of service and sacrifice; of tragedy and triumph; of camaraderie in the face of overwhelming challenges. From Presidents to community activists and artists to generals, our collective history is full of stories of people who fought for change, or perhaps for peace and justice, because they loved our country and believed it was worth fighting for.

No other group of Americans, however, has stood more bravely for our democracy than our veterans. The stories of our veterans, their families and the civilians who supported them are the story of our nation's perseverance and commitment to the ideals of democracy and freedom. In troubled times, our veterans tell a story not just of hardship and courage, but of hope and opportunity. Each one has a story to tell us.

Unfortunately, of the more than 2.5 million WWII veterans living in the United States today, we lose about 900 every day.

That's why it's so important to have their personal experiences recorded in volumes like this one. Having first-hand accounts of the experiences of all war veterans, as well as the civilians who supported them, and how it fits into the entire fabric of our nation's history is vital if future generations of Americans are to fully understand our history.

I'm proud to join in this effort to show my appreciation for the ordinary heroes among us.

Dennis Moore
Member of Congress

ACKNOWLEDGEMENTS

I would like to extend my gratitude to the men and women whose stories appear in this book. These men and women graciously welcomed me into their homes and allowed me to interview and record, in their words, a very indelible period of their lives; and trusted me to return their valuable photographs which were more than fifty and sixty years old. Some of these men and women allowed me to utilize information from their unpublished, and published, written accounts.

Five of the stories which appear in this book, were written for *The Best Times* where they first appeared in print. *The Best Times,* edited by Lynn Anderson, is a monthly publication of Aging Information & Action of Johnson County, Kansas, in partnership with the Area Agency on Aging, a division of Johnson County Human Services & Aging. Those five stories are accounts given by Albert Henke, Earl McCabe, Bob Jackson, Ben Lohman and Christl Upchurch.

A special thanks is extended to Albert Henke, Francis Medina, Dorinda Nicholson and Christl Upchurch for allowing me to use their published books to write their stories. Information about their publications and how they may be obtained are listed at the end of their stories. Thanks to Matthew T. Davidson, whose young and healthy eyes scrutinized the final draft of the manuscript; and to Dwight Staples for discovering computer glitches. Thanks, also, to Kim Pardon who helped computerize the final draft for submission to the publishing house.

As always, I owe a big debt of thanks to my wife, Marian, for her ideas, suggestions, support, proof reading and patience while the following pages were being written.

TABLE OF CONTENTS

	Page	
Foreword		iii
Acknowledgements		iv

Book I
Prisoners of War

Chapter 1.....Paul Bosworth: B-17 ball gunner/POW		2
2...."Nick" Gettino: B-24 navigator/POW		13
3....Robert Jackson: B-17 navigator/POW who returned to crash site		20
4....Lee Lamar: B-24 Pilot/POW who returned to crash site		32
5...."Ben" Lohman: Marine/POW		40

Book II
Children Prisoners of War

6....Betsy Heimke: POW	46
7....Frank Saunders: POW	59

Book III
Children under Fire

8....Dorinda Nicholson: Pearl Harbor	72
9....Christl Upchurch: Schweinfurt, Germany	83
10...Hubert Manthe: Hitler Youth member	95

Book IV
Underground Evasion

11...."Frank" Medina: Italy	106
12....Nikolas Willems: The Netherlands	121

Book V
Proud to Serve

13.... "Bill" Davis: P-51 ace	134
14....Vernon Davy: Sailor LCT	142
15....Dan Fedynich: B-17 ball gunner	150
16....Sally Hatch: British soldier	157

17....Albert Henke: B-17 tail gunner	167
18....Earl McCabe: Marine F4U Pilot	176
19....Leonard Porter: USAF career pilot	180

Book VI
Vietnam

20....Peter Illman: Marine	192
21....Kathy Lee: Combat Nurse	199

Book VII
Letters Home

22....Lloyd Langdon: Combat Pilot/KIA	213
23....Lest we forget: Some last letters home	226
24....Photographs of the major aircraft mentioned in the chapters	236

BOOK I

Prisoners of War

Chapter 1

Paul H. Bosworth
B-17 Tail gunner & POW

November 28, 1925 was one of those cold, wind-blown winter evenings in Chicago, when a physician received an emergency call to the Grant Hospital to deliver a baby. The physician, busy enjoying Chicago's nightlife, rushed to the hospital as fast as he could and skillfully brought Paul H. Bosworth into the world while still attired in his tuxedo.

Bosworth grew up in Chicago and attended Waters Elementary School, and graduated from Lane Tech High School. Since Bosworth's father owned two "filling stations," Bosworth worked many hours during his high school years servicing automobiles; "after," according to Bosworth, "I finished my homework."

Bosworth joins the US Army

By 1943, Bosworth's two older brothers were serving their country in uniform. One was a Marine Corps pilot, and the other was in the US Army. Bosworth was itching to go into the US Navy's V-5 pilot training program to become a naval aviator. A minor problem with his eyes, however, scuttled his chances for pilot training. Bosworth persisted, and in early 1944 joined the US Army with very serious intentions of being around airplanes. He volunteered to be an aerial gunner.

Bosworth reported to Miami, Florida were he was assigned to quarters at the Evans Hotel. He remembers the hotel well because of an incident in which he suggested to a sergeant a better way to do something (he doesn't remember what). He does remember, however, that the sergeant didn't appreciate his advice, and assigned him to clean the lobby floor with a toothbrush.

From Miami, Bosworth was sent to Kingman Army Air Base in Arizona to receive training as a gunner. "I shot a lot of cacti while there," remembers Bosworth. From Kingman, Bosworth traveled to MacDill Field in Tampa, Florida where he assembled with others to form a bomber crew. His crew flew their practice flights in the Boeing B-17 Flying Fortress. According to Bosworth, "I loved that airplane from the very first. It was a great ship."

In early December of 1944, Bosworth's crew left MacDill for their journey to England to become part of the raging war in Europe. They loaded their factory-new B-17 with all of their gear and took off for England. Bosworth was in awe of the spectacular view as his Flying Fortress soared over Charleston, Philadelphia, New York City and Connecticut before landing near Manchester, New Hampshire.

After stops in Labrador and Ireland they landed in Wales. From there a train transported them to England for more training. Bosworth and his crew arrived at their permanent base in Chelveston, England. Bosworth's crew was assigned to the Eight Air Force, 305th Bomb Group, and the 366th Squadron. He and his fellow enlisted men were able to find living quarters in a Quonset hut. "The countryside was very picturesque," remembers Bosworth.

Combat flying

Earlier, when the pilot of Bosworth's crew asked Bosworth which position as gunner he preferred (tail, waist or ball "belly"); Bosworth chose the tail gunner's position. Those who were assigned a bombing mission were usually awakened at 3:00 A.M. for breakfast and briefings. By 6:00 A.M. they traveled to their airplanes to load their gear and check-out their particular positions. By 7:30 A.M. the crew was ready for take off. The bombers took off in 30 second intervals, climbed to between 1,500 to 3,000 feet and circled while the other bombers formed-up in formation with them. When the formation reached the English Channel, they climbed to 23,000 feet and headed toward Germany.

Since higher altitudes reached 30 to 60 degrees below zero, crew members wore two or three layers of clothing, gloves, head gear and an electric flight suit. With oxygen masks and goggles, very little of the crewman's face was exposed. After the mission, the crews were debriefed, asked questions about the bomb run, given a shot of whiskey and sent to evening chow. Most of the days were long and fatiguing.

Bosworth's first combat mission was to Koblenz, Germany. The mission had fighter protection, and the B-17s did not have to duke-it-out with the Luftwaffe's deadly fighters. There was plenty of flak over the target. "...of course you're frightened," recalls Bosworth. "You can't help but be frightened because you're so horribly concerned about what you are going to do? Who will crawl back here if I get hit? How can I get up there if somebody's hurt?" After landing from the first mission, no bullet or flak holes were found on the aircraft.

Bosworth's second mission was much like the first. But this time, holes were discovered on the airplane after landing. When a bomber was down for repairs or maintenance, the flight crews were assigned other aircraft for a mission. On one occasion, Bosworth's crew was assigned the famous *Memphis Belle* for a mission. "Of course," stated Bosworth, "we had no idea at that time that the airplane would become so famous."

After about six missions or so, Bosworth began to be more relaxed in the tail position of the Fortress. The typical position for a tail gunner was to enter and sit on a bicycle seat that was extended up from the floor. Once the gunner sat on the bicycle seat, he would be on his knees with his feet tucked back underneath him. Kneeling in that position for as many as six to 12 hours was extremely tiring. Bosworth developed his own position. He would sit on the bicycle seat, stretch his legs out in front of him, and lean his back against a vertical rod behind him. He found this position to be much more comfortable and less tiring than the recommended way. The vertical rod on which Bosworth leaned was the airplane's rudder shaft. The pilot knew it, but didn't disapprove.

On Bosworth's 14th mission he was sitting comfortably in his new-found position. For some reason, he decided to sit in the kneeling position for awhile. The kneeling position caused his head to move forward. At that time a bullet came through one side of the airplane, and out the other side. If Bosworth had been sitting back in his favorite position, the bullet would have gone through one side of his head and out the other.

Bosworth is shot down

The morning of March 2, 1945 didn't get off to a good start. Bosworth's crew overslept their 3:00 A.M. wakeup call and had to be called a second time. They missed some of their briefings and had to finish dressing in the airplane.

The mission was to bomb a ball bearing plant in Bohlen, Germany near Dresden. Bosworth's squadron was leading over 1000 planes against "...one of the most heavily concentrated flak areas I had ever seen," Bosworth later recalled. Bosworth's B-17 was carrying 250 pound anti-personnel bombs.

Most bomb runs, during the time the bombers align themselves with the target and stay on a straight and level course, last from five to seven minutes. It is a harrowing time when the anti-aircraft guns can more easily place the bombers in their line of fire, and gauge their altitude while the bomber moves straight ahead hoping it will not be hit. Bosworth felt this bomb run was exceptionally long—fifteen minutes, at least.

While on the final run, Bosworth reported to the pilot that oil was streaming along the right side of the airplane. He heard a "clunking" noise. Number three engine had been hit and there wasn't enough oil in it to even feather the prop, and the unfeathered prop was causing the B-17 to shake dramatically. The pilot was finally able to shear the prop loose by performing a violent stall. The crew dropped their bombs in order to lighten the load for the three engines left, and dropped from formation. But then, number one engine began coughing and showing signs of failure. The pilot decided to head for Russia for safety, but the navigator had forgotten the maps.

But when number one engine cleared up, the pilot decided that with three and one half hours of fuel left, they might be able to make the four hours it took to get to France if they further lightened their load. The crew threw everything out of the airplane they could get loose, including the ball turret. The airplane, which had been flying at about 150 mph, at 29,000 feet, was now down to about 12,000 feet, because their oxygen system was shot up. Soon, flak hit the waist gun positions. As they passed over the Rhein, still flying west they were hit by flak again.

The B-17 was slowly losing altitude. Bosworth and two other gunners looked outside the crippled Fortress and saw two German Me109s at about eye level. Bosworth was sure that, "This is it." The enemy fighters bore in on the disabled Flying Fortress. They made two close passes right by the bomber and then flew off in the distance. Either the fighters were out of ammunition, or they decided to let the Americans live. As the bomber, at about 1,500 feet, passed over Frankfurt, Germany it took more flak. The navigator didn't seem to know exactly where they were.

The situation was dire. The crew had made preparations to bail out. The pilot circled over what he thought was friendly territory in France; and gave the signal to bail out. The crewmen began to bail out. When the waist gunner positioned himself in the door way to jump, he just stood. Bosworth, who was behind him, knew the airplane was loosing altitude. They had to get out fast. Bosworth finally put his foot on the hesitant man and booted him out of the plane. The man's parachute opened only seconds before he touched down. All of the crew bailed safely, except the pilot. He never left the airplane.

Bosworth becomes a POW

Bosworth and four other crewmembers landed in the same vicinity. Suddenly the downed airmen looked up and saw several German civilians running toward them with axes, pitchforks and knives. It was common knowledge that civilians who suffered terribly from the Allied bombings would kill American and British airmen when they caught them on the ground. They surrounded Bosworth's group, and seemed to be waiting for a signal to act. It was scary.

The tension was broken by a German soldier running down the hill shouting at the top of his lungs, "Achtung! Achtung!" (Attention! Attention!). He began talking to the German civilians, and suddenly they left. Then the German soldier turned to Bosworth's group, and in English, told them his story.

The soldier had been captured and spent two years as an American POW at the Fitzsimmons General Hospital in Denver, Colorado. He had just recently been repatriated back to Germany. He had been sitting on a hill with his lady friend when he heard the B-17. He had seen Bosworth's crew bail out, and knew that there was going to be trouble, so he ran down the hill to the group as fast as he could. He told the Americans that when the war was over that he would like to return to the United States and become an American citizen.

The German soldier had saved the American fliers' lives. When Bosworth's group asked the German soldier to let them go, he replied, "I just can't do that." The soldier took them to the nearest town where they were locked-up in a jail. It was then that Bosworth's crew found that they had bailed out over the beautiful, old Roman city of Trier, Germany. Bosworth and his crew were put in a jail in the city. By seeing to it that Bosworth was placed in the relatively safety of a POW camp, the soldier, may again, have saved Bosworth's life.

That evening Bosworth was marched to a train station and transported to Kirchberg, Germany where he was held in solitary confinement in a cold cell for five days. For breakfast he was given tea, and for supper he was given two slices of sour black bread and a bowl of potato soup. At the end of the five days, the POWs were placed in box cars and made their way to an Interrogation Center in Wetzler, Germany. The box cars were crowded. They received no food while on the train. They traveled only by night, out of fear of being destroyed by Allied aircraft during the day.

At Wetzler, Bosworth was held in a windowless, cold cell which measured five by eight feet. He slept on a wooden board with one thin blanket. In the morning he was fed some kind of goulash, and for supper he had black bread. But he was hungry—and he devoured it.

On the fifth day of confinement, Bosworth was taken from his cell for interrogation. Once in the interrogation room, Bosworth sat in front of a desk occupied by a German officer. When the German officer asked Bosworth if there was anything that Bosworth wanted to say to him; Bosworth said, "Yes. My name is Paul Bosworth. My serial number is 36901671, and I'm in the Army Air Corps—

period." The German officer just laughed. Then he took out a file and told Bosworth, "Your dad owns two gas stations on Western Avenue in the city of Chicago, just two blocks from Lane Tech High School where you and your two brothers went to school. There are more things. You can't help me much. So, stand up, salute me, and leave." Bosworth was astounded.

The next day Bosworth boarded a train and endured another miserable three days until he reached Nüremberg. At Nüremberg Bosworth was placed in a POW compound that was once used as a Hitler Youth camp. The POWs lived in tents and were fed two meals a day.

March to Mooseburg

After 21 days, the Germans decided to move 10,000 of the POWs to another POW compound near Mooseburg. The POWs would march the 80 miles in 16 days to get there. As they marched away from Nüremberg, they watched, as allied bombs fell on the city behind them.

On one of the days during the march, four American fighters appeared. The two P-47s and the two P-51s rolled over and lined up to attack what they thought were German troops. The first fighter strafed the men and dropped two bombs. The second airplane strafed, but dropped no bombs. The other two just made a low pass. Evidently, an American colonel in the POW march held an American flag up, and the pilots saw it. Later during the march, the fighters returned. Sometimes they just circled above to give the POWs confidence. Sometimes they just made low passes, which thrilled the marching POWs.

"Mooseburg was a filthy place," recalls Bosworth. "We were placed in tents that ordinarily housed 30 men and now held 100. We had to stay in groups of ten." The guards ranged in age from 30 to 75. The POWs slept on wooden planks which they placed branches on to dull the hardness. Morale was low and some of the POWs would quarrel. The men gave each other hair cuts using a tin lid from a can. If one did not hold too many strands of hair in his hand, the tin can would finally cut the hair by sawing back and forth. Bosworth made a spoon from an old tin can lid, a small piece of wood and some wire. He used it every day to eat his soup, and still has it to this day.

Bosworth is liberated

On April 28, 1945, there seemed to be a tense atmosphere in the camp. It was quiet. There were no German guards in sight. The POWs wondered if the Allied armies were near the camp. POWs who had been with the infantry, told their fellow prisoners that they would know that our army was near when they heard the sounds of the big guns and heavy artillery. That night Bosworth heard the loud sounds of the big guns. Early the next morning, Bosworth saw the jeeps and tanks, with the beautiful white stars on their sides, of General George Patton's 14th Armored Division enter the camp. The music emanating from a radio in one of the jeeps was one of the most wonderful sounds that the POWs had heard for a long, long time.

There were no shots fired. Patton had negotiated with the German camp commander. Patton told the commander that if he and the camp staff and guards walked away quietly on the evening of the 28th, he would not harm them. And the next morning Patton would move in. That is exactly what happened.

The POWs awakened on the next morning to see 55 gallon drums filled with good American coffee, and Patton's men were cooking breakfast. The POWs were ecstatic. Men were "crying like babies." By noon the flag of the United States of America was flying over the Mooseburg POW compound. They were free.

Bosworth lost 20 pounds during the two months he was held prisoner. "If it hadn't been for the American Red Cross boxes, we would have starved," Bosworth believes.

Bosworth remained at the POW compound for about eight days before he and his buddies were loaded onto army trucks and transported to Landshut, Germany were they were to board C-47s. The POWs were told that they could go into the town of Landshut if they liked; but they should return at a certain time or be left behind.

Bosworth and his best buddy, Byron Crum, went to town. The Crum family had been friends with the Bosworth family before the war. As teenagers, Bosworth and Crum had been friends. The two boys entered the army at about the same time. Crum was the radio operator on Bosworth's crew, and of course, they were shot down together. They remained friends throughout their POW captivity; and Bosworth and Crum, and their wives, remained friends after the war until Crum's death in 2003.

In town the two young men walked around just gawking. They walked into a garage where a few beautiful automobiles were parked. They decided to take one and drive it back to the base. They were stymied in their attempt, however, because none of the cars had batteries. While walking down the street, they saw a motorcycle parked by a curb. On the front of the motorcycle was a beautifully colored plate with a German swastika and eagle on it. Upon closer examination, the plate looked loose. Bosworth removed it as a souvenir, and still has it to this day.

On May 8, 1945 (V-E Day), Bosworth left Germany to go to Camp Lucky Strike in LeHarve, France. At Lucky Strike he was deloused. He enjoyed the bath, since he had had only two baths since he parachuted from the B-17. He and Crum were told to put goggles on while they were sprayed with DDT to get rid of the scabies.

On May 29th, the ship *Thomas H. Perry* unloaded Bosworth at Staten Island, New York. The men boarded ferries that took them past the Statue of Liberty. Bosworth remembers that joyous moment, "…that brought tears to every man's eyes." Bosworth was elated to be home. He regained some weight and cherished his freedom. He has indelible memories of the shot-up B-17, and his POW days. Sometimes he awakens in the night thinking about some of those moments; but he harbors no animosity toward the German people.

Bosworth received his discharge on December 7, 1945. In 1947 he married his prewar girl friend, Shirley Lee, to whom he was married for 58 years before her death. Shirley and Paul had three children, and two grandchildren. He ended his working career as a successful salesman for printing supplies.

LEFT: Crum (left) and Bosworth. **RIGHT:** Bosworth and Shirley Lee before they were married.

Bosworth's POW I.D. tag & the plate he took off of the motorcycle in Landshut. The spoon Bosworth made to eat soup.

 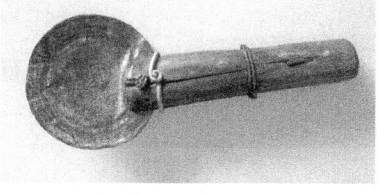

POW Camp at Nüremberg.

Paul H. Bosworth: 2008

Chapter 2

Nick Gettino
B-24 Navigator & POW

Background

Nick Gettino, the son of a restaurant owner, was born in Syracuse, New York, and was raised in the small village of Solvay, New York. Gettino was a superb athlete and lettered every year in high school in football, baseball and basketball (12 letters total). He was also involved in track.

A football scholarship took him to Belmont Abbey College in North Carolina, and later to George Washington University in Washington, D.C. After busting up his shoulder, and sustaining other injuries, he transferred to Tri-State University in Angola, Indiana where he pursued a degree in mechanical engineering.

Gettino had a high interest in airplanes, and made models since he was eleven years old. He enlisted in the USAAF in 1942 but was not called until 1943.

Gettino becomes a pilot

Gettino began his training at Sheppard Field in Texas. He logged about 60 hours in the PT-19 before he washed out of pilot training and, subsequently, was shipped to San Marco, Texas to begin his training in navigation.

Gettino completed his training and was assigned as a navigator on a B-24. Shortly afterward, Gettino and his newly formed crew boarded a train for Topeka, Kansas. At Topeka, the crew was assigned a brand new B-24 Liberator bomber.

Happy to have their own airplane, the crew wasted no time in deciding a name for their war machine; they christened it *My Sad Ass*. A large donkey was painted on each side of the nose. The donkey was turned in a manner so that he was looking at his rear, which was painted red. The caption under the colorful nose art read: *My Melancholy Rectum.*

Since Topeka was to be the *My Sad Asses'* last pause before heading for an overseas assignment, the crew was allowed to invite their family, wives or girlfriends to Topeka.

Gettino's mother and father visited him, and at Gettino's request, brought along his sweetheart, Mary Bums. The fire in the hearts of both Gettino and Bums must have been turned to high, because when Gettino *popped the question;* Bums said, "Yes."

Overseas assignment

The flight to their overseas destination was a long one. Touching down in Florida, Puerto Rico (where they stayed for 15 days to repair a fuel tank), British Guyana and Brazil; they took off for the 2200 mile flight to Ekenes Air Base at Dakar in French West Africa.

Gettino navigated the flight by taking wave readings from the swells of the Atlantic, and shot fixes from the sun and stars. "It was quite nerve racking," recalls Gettino. Gettino hit his destination right on the nose. This expert job of navigating won for Gettino the trust and admiration from his crew. They landed with 25 gallons of gas remaining in the tanks of their Liberator. On May 29th Gettino and his crew arrived at San Pancrazio in Southern Italy where they were assigned to the 15th Air Force, 376th Bomb Group, 515th squadron.

Air combat

On June 4, 1944, about six days after his arrival, Gettino flew his first combat mission to the marshalling yards in Genoa, Italy. Two days later (D-Day) Gettino flew his second mission. It was a harrowing mission to Ploesti. Six Me109s attacked Gettino's B-24. When the tail gunner threw his firepower at them at 500 yards, the Me109s scattered and came in again under the B-24's belly. One Me109 shot down Gettino's wing man, but Gettino's belly turret gunner shot the Me109 and sent him diving away smoking. The

B-24s tightened formation. Two B-24s were shot down, and two men on the other B-24s were killed.

On Gettino's third mission to Treiste, they lost one engine, and another engine was acting up. On Gettino's fourth mission their B-24 again had to land with only three engines.

On another raid to the oil fields of Ploesti, Gettino's formation was attacked by 50 Me109s. Two of the gunners in Gettino's crew each shot an Me109 down. A B-24 on Gettino's wing was hit, the wing came off and it went down in a ball of flames. Only three parachutes were seen. "It was a sickening sight," remembers Gettino.

On a mission to Toulon, flak knocked out the nose wheel of Gettino's airplane. The B-24 spun down to 3000 feet before leveling. They made a forced landing on Anzio Beach Head. As on most of Gettino's missions, there were several holes in the airplane.

On the way home from a bomb run over Budapest, Gettino's radio operator had a complete mental breakdown. He wasn't the only man in the squadron to *break* from the stress of combat. By September 4, 1944 Gettino had flown 33 combat missions in 92 days. His bomb runs included targets (many of them two or three times) in: Zagreb, Sisak, Borovnica, and Krajevo, Yugoslavia; Forli, and Brecia, Italy; Toulon, Nice, Servano, and St Tropez, France; Budapest, Hungary; Giurgiu, Ploesti, Romania; St. Polten, Vienna, and Szegred, Austria; and Friedrichshafen, Germany. He flew at least three missions over the Ploesti oil fields.

During these 92 days Gettino witnessed very heavy, thick flak, and they were attacked many times by Me109s and Fw190s. He saw many aircraft shot down, including the horrid sight of B-24s, and he saw planes collide. His aircraft made it back to base at least three times on one engine. Landing at an alternative field on one occasion, the whole crew was listed as Missing-In-Action.

The policy of the 15th Air Force for the Heavy Bomber Groups was to allow a week's Rest and Recreation (R & R) on the island of Capri after a crew had completed 34 combat missions.

On September 4, 1944 Gettino had completed his 33rd combat mission. A B-24 scheduled for a mission on September 8th had to be scratched because of mechanical problems. Gettino's crew heard about the cancellation. They also heard that the mission for which it was scheduled was a *milk run* (meaning an easy mission with less flak and enemy fighter opposition). The reasoning of Gettino's crew was that after completing an easy 34th mission, they could then go on R & R.

Shot down

On September 8, 1944 Gettino's crew, loaded with forty 500 pound bombs, took off to bomb the railroad yards in Nis, Yugoslavia. The crew had an uneventful two hours to the target. They passed the initial point, and opened the bomb bay doors. Even then, few flak bursts were seen. The bombs were dropped. "At that time," recalls Gettino, "all hell broke loose. We took a direct hit on our number two engine.... The concussion blew us out of the formation, and we began to dive."

The plane was smoking and sparks were flying in every direction. Gettino opened the nose wheel emergency door and bailed out. According to Gettino, "It was a long way down." During his decent he saw three other parachutes, and watched his B-24 smoking as it disappeared from his sight. Unfortunately, Gettino's parachute straps were too loose, and his legs and arms were jerked furiously when his chute jerked open. He was paralyzed and bleeding.

The wind was blowing him back toward the town he had just bombed. As he floated earthward, he saw five soldiers waiting for him to land. Gettino landed on his back and two of the soldiers immediately jumped on him, while another one drew his bayonet. "I thought it was over," recalls Gettino. One soldier cut his parachute straps with the bayonet. Two soldiers held Gettino while two other soldiers kicked and hit him. They broke his nose and his jaw. Blood was running from his nose and his mouth; his legs were numb from the jump. They also took his navigation watch.

Gettino becomes a POW

A German officer drove up to the scene and ordered the beating to stop. The German officer saluted Gettino, which Gettino returned. Then, in perfect English, the German officer said, "I apologize for these soldiers' conduct."

The German officer later bummed a cigarette from Gettino and told him that he had visited his aunt in Milwaukee and how he had enjoyed driving her Oldsmobile.

Gettino was placed in a vehicle, and as he was driven back to an airport in the town, he observed the numerous fires and the devastation which his mission of B-24s and P-38s had wrought. When he arrived at the airport, he was reunited with his bombardier, Paul Kiecker.

Shortly afterward, Gettino and Kiecker were loaded into railroad cars where they slept on filthy hay. Before reaching Budapest, they had to evacuate the train for awhile because of allied strafing.

The train stopped before reaching Budapest, and Gettino was marched through the streets of the town to a prison. Along the way, the population of the town yelled and cursed at the prisoners.

The only reason they were not killed was because of the protection afforded to them by the German guards who cocked their guns and trained them on the townspeople.

For approximately two weeks, Gettino was interrogated daily. He received threats of being shot and/or being hanged. The prisoners lived through terrible British bombing raids.

His cell was 4 feet by 6 feet. It had a toilet and some straw on the floor for a bed. His food consisted of small servings of bread which was chased down by water.

Finally, Gettino and other POWs were loaded into trucks and delivered to Stalag Lufte III in Sagan (Zagan) Germany. Upon arrival, he was deloused and gloried in his first shower in two months.

At the Stalag Lufte III, which was a POW camp primarily for allied airmen, Gettino lived in cramped quarters with a burlap bag filled with straw for a mattress.

Twice a week he would receive one cup of barley or potato soup and one dark loaf of heavy bread which was divided among 15 POWs. The *black bread,* as it was called, was made of many things, including sawdust and tiny pieces of glass. The *blood sausage* they sometimes were served amounted to sausage skins filled with the blood of dead animals. Sometimes, their meals were supplemented by parcels of food from the Red Cross.

Because the Russian thrust into Germany was rolling at full speed, and was only 30 miles away from the POW camp, the Germans decided to move the POWs to another location. On January, 28, 1945, a little after midnight, when it was snowing and the temperature was zero degrees, the POWs began their march.

After seven days and 62 miles of insufferable conditions, the prisoners were loaded into crowded boxcars and shipped to a POW camp, Stalag VII, near Mooseburg. According to Gettino, "This was a hell hole."

Liberation
On April 29, 1944 the POW camp was liberated by allied forces. Gettino and a buddy hooked up with a couple of soldiers who shot a deer. They took it into town and a German lady cooked it for them. It was Gettino's first meal in eight months. Gettino, whose normal weight was 190 pounds, weighed 140 pounds.

Gettino finally arrived in La Harve, France on V-E Day, and back to his hometown in New York on June 7, 1945. Gettino married his sweetheart, Mary, the following month, and after 61 years, seven children and 14 grandchildren, they are still married.

After the war Gettino returned to Tri-State College and completed his degree in civil engineering.

He was employed by Curtis-Wright where he worked on the XP-87 jet, and spent some time working for chemical companies. He was employed by General Electric in the military where he worked on aircraft radar, and later Syracuse University where he worked on the EA6-A Intruder and back to G.E. where he retired. Gettino followed three of his children to Kansas, two of whom, attended Kansas State University.

Reported Missing, Lt. Gettino Safe

Lt. Nicholas A. Gettino, son of Mr. and Mrs. Samuel Gettino of 2615 Milton ave., Solvay, who was reported missing in action on June 25, wrote a letter to his parents after the war department telegram saying that his plane had been forced to land on water. After five days the crew of the B-24 Liberator returned uninjured to their base in Italy.

Lt. N. A. Gettino

Gettino, a navigator, has been promoted to first lieutenant. He entered service two years ago while attending Tri-State university, Indiana. He received his wings Feb. 5 at the army air forces navigation school, San Marcos, Tex.

A brother, Richard, who was graduated as a dentist in June from Marquette university, Wisconsin, is awaiting orders into the dental corps.

FREE 110,000 AT MOSSBURG

Third Army Liberates Largest Prison Camp in Reich

WITH THE UNITED STATES THIRD ARMY, in Germany, April 30 (AP)—The United States Fourteenth Armored Division liberated 110,000 Allied prisoners of war at Stalag 7A at Mossburg, instead of the 27,000 previously reported. This was Germany's biggest prisoner of war camp.

The roster included the names of 11,000 Americans. There also were Britons, South Africans, New Zealanders, Australians, Poles, Russians, Frenchmen and Yugoslavs, and some war correspondents. The first accounts gave no names.

The Mossburg camp was taken by the Fourteenth Armored Division's Forty-seventh Tank Battalion, which found nineteen of its own troops there.

Nick Gettino in front of B-24

Satan's Kids
376th B. G.

Chapter 3

Bob Jackson
POW Returns to Crash Site in France

The renowned *Life* magazine photographer, Margaret Bourke-White, had visited the military air base in Petersburg, England with the express purpose of taking photographs of military personnel which would graphically bring scenes of the far away war home to Americans.

Standing among the ten man flight crew of the B-17 which Margaret Bourke-White photographed was 22 year old, 6' 2", Bob Jackson, who hailed from a small town in Iowa. That particular issue of *Life* magazine, with the premium photograph of the young flyers, hit the newstands on October 19, 1942. Two days later, none of the ten airmen in the photograph returned from their mission that day. Their Flying Fortress had been shot down by a Focke-Wulf 190 German fighter.

The mission

Lt. Bob Jackson was a navigator on the world famous Boeing B-17 Flying Fortress, attached to the Eighth Air Force, 97th Bomb Group. Jackson had survived five combat missions flying through the flak-filled skies over Europe dropping bombs on German submarine pens (submarine bases) and enemy rail yards.

The bombing mission for October 21, 1942 was scheduled for a mid-morning takeoff.

The target for the day was the heavily reinforced concrete Nazi submarine pens near Lorient in Brittany, France, which intelligence had reported, were the headquarters of the German U-boats in the Atlantic.

Jackson's crew climbed into their B-17, *The Big Bitch*, and readied their gear for combat and high altitude freezing temperatures. The history behind the name of their airplane is rather simple. Most young men in the military sometimes gripe, complain and bitch. According to Jackson, his crew was a big bunch of gripers, and bitchers. Thus, the name of the airplane was a ludicrous reference to the crew—*The Big Bitch*. After the signal for takeoff, *The Big Bitch* clawed for altitude and formed into a V formation with two other Fortresses, as it joined with the other 89 heavy bombers assigned to the mission.

Aerial combat

Once across the English Channel, the bomber's fighter escort turned back, and the bombers were on their own. The bombers saw the Luftwaffe (German Air Force) Fw-190s, close to 40, waiting for them over France. The German fighters attacked the bombers in waves. Jackson, who was positioned in the Plexiglas nose, witnessed the fighters roaring toward him with their guns firing. Then suddenly, the fighters rolled over on their backs and disappeared under the B-17.

The Big Bitch was over the village of Saint Vougay, France when the first wave of fighters destroyed their internal communication system. The second wave was so destructive that Capt. John Bennett, the pilot, gave the order for the crew to bail out. Bennett bailed out; Jackson remembers only the explosion. He does not remember pulling the rip cord that would open his parachute. He believes that a crew member pulled the rip cord and shoved him out of the airplane—a crew member who did not live through the jump himself.

Within minutes, Jackson was lying on the ground unconscious, with breaks in his knee, shoulder, and hips. Even today, Jackson feels the results of those injuries. The German soldiers who found him hauled him to a nearby infirmary in some poor farmer's confiscated potato cart. Jackson and Bennett were the only survivors of the ten-man crew.

Prisoner of War

After a few days Jackson was transferred to a former American hospital in Paris. He remembers looking out of his hospital room window at the Eiffel Tower. He also remembers a German officer asking him if all Americans were as big as he. He also remembers three German flyers, who in the flyers' world of camaraderie, wanted to meet him and shake his hand. After about ten days Jackson was well enough to walk with crutches, and was transferred to a prison camp.

After being kept in solitary confinement, and interrogated for two days at the camp, Jackson was transferred to Stalag Luft III in Sagan, Germany (now Zagan, Poland) which was about 100 miles south of Berlin. He would be incarcerated as a POW for the next two a half years. As time wore on, and shortages of food were pervasive throughout Germany and her occupied territories, the POWs were fed less and less. All of the POWs lost weight.

The *Great Escape*

Stalag Luft III was a prison camp primarily for allied flyers. In most cases the Americans and British flyers were separated into their own sections. Jackson, and Bennett who later joined him, were among a small group of Americans in the British section.

One day word circulated among the prisoners that if they wanted to dig tunnels for an escape attempt, they should sign up for the soccer teams in the prison. "Escaping was sort of a game," recalls Jackson. "Escaping was a duty without arms." The whole operation was planned and organized by the British POWs.

The escape plan has drawn world wide attention because of Paul Brickhill, an Australian with the Royal Australian Air Force, who was a POW in Stalag Luft III with Jackson. Brickhill published a detailed account of the incident in 1950 titled *The Great Escape*. In 1963 a movie was made using the same title starring Steve McQueen.

The basic plan of the escape involved digging three separate tunnels, 24 feet beneath the prison yard, and 300 feet long to extend beyond the fence into the woods. Jackson not only helped dig tunnels, he also helped dispose of the dirt. Both jobs were dangerous and involved ingenious methods of execution.

Before the tunnels were completed, Jackson and the other Americans were transferred from the British section to an American section. Consequently, Jackson was not able to participate in the escape; and that is probably why he is still alive today. In March of 1944, of the 77 prisoners who escaped the prison, only three evaded capture by the German guards. Fifty of those were gunned-downed by the Germans after capture.

Because the Russian Army was progressing toward Stalag Luft III, the Germans decided to evacuate the POWs. Jackson was in the group that was forced to march over three nights in bitterly cold weather. Food was scarce, and many of the men's feet froze. Finally, after being packed into box cars like sardines, they arrived at Staling VII-A near Moosberg, Germany.

On April 28, 1945, when Jackson had been at Stalag VII-A for only three months, a tank company from General Patton's Third Army liberated the camp. The commander of the unit had been a classmate of Jackson's at Morningside College in Sioux City, Iowa.

Lingering memories

Jackson left the military after the war in order to pursue the American dream. He married, became a commercial painter, raised a family; and now lives in Olathe, Kansas. Those memories of an explosion high over the skies of France, and the POW years in Germany have lingered in his thoughts all of his life.

The only two survivors of the ten man crew, Jackson and his pilot John Bennett, remained friends, and called each other every year on October the 21st, the anniversary of the day they were blasted out of the sky. Bennett passed away in 1991, and Jackson is the only living member of *The Big Bitch's* crew.

On April 13, 2006 Jackson's telephone rang in his Olathe home. The person on the other end of the line told Jackson that they were relatives of one of his crew members who had been killed on that fateful day. They were surprised, they said, to learn that a survivor existed; and they said that they had some information in which he may be interested. "I was absolutely shocked," recalls Jackson.

The search for *The Big Bitch's* survivors

The startling telephone call which Jackson answered on April 13, 2006 in his home in Olathe was the result of some dogged, time-consuming research performed by Rodney and Destia Hermes of Redman, Washington. Rodney was a cousin of Thomas Morgan, the bombardier on Jackson's B-17 when it was shot down near the village of Saint Vougay, France on October 21, 1942. Morgan was one of the eight crew members who did not survive the disaster. Hermes, five years old at the time, remembers only the tears and sorrow of family members brought about by the young flyer's death.

Hermes's wife, Destia, is of French descent, and has taught French in American schools. The Hermes visits their time-share apartment in France annually. A few years back the Hermes began to research the crash site and the crew members of *The Big Bitch*. Research quickly revealed that only the pilot, John Bennett, and the navigator, Bob Jackson, lived. The burning question harbored in their minds was, "Where are these men?"

Research revealed that Bennett had lived in Colorado, and Jackson had lived in Iowa upon their enlistment into the USAAF. Since Jackson had been gone from Estherville, Iowa, and no relatives remained in the town; the Hermes' research reached a dead end.

Finally, the Hermes reached Bennett's widow in Colorado by telephone who said, "Well, you should be talking to Bob Jackson; I have his address and telephone number." Bingo! The Hermes hit the jackpot. According to Jackson, "When I answered the phone that day and identified himself, I heard Destia saying to the people in the room on the other end of the line, 'It's him! It's him! It's him!'"

A plan to honor Jackson is conceived

For about a year and a half after the 2006 telephone call, e-mails and letters between the United States and France crossed the Atlantic Ocean, most all of them in French. Involved in the communications, to note a few: were the President of the French Republic, the French Ambassador to the United States, the United

States Ambassador to France, the Mayor of Saint Vouguay, and Destia Hermes.

Jackson gathered his military records (discharge papers, unit information and dates) and mailed them to the French Embassy. The whole process of verification took months to assimilate and verify. In a letter to the French General Counselor, the Charge d'affaire, Laurent Delahouse, of the French Embassy wrote (as translated from French by local resident Renee Davis), "I did notice…that Mr. Jackson is eligible for a nomination in the Order of the Legion of Honor, and I am entirely ready to present his candidature to the Grand Chancellery."

In 2006, the Hermes, after returning from a trip to France, brought a piece of the wing of *The Big Bitch* to Jackson which he proudly displays on a wall in his home. The piece of wing had belonged to a farmer in the area of Saint Vougay who had found it in a field and had nailed it on his barn to cover a hole.

The crowning achievement to the months of exhaustive process of letter writing and record scavenging resulted in a trip for Jackson to return to France to be honored by the French. Jackson and his good friend, Dwayne Lagerstrum, a 66 year old retiree, would depart Kansas City, Missouri for Paris, France on October 16, 2007.

Revisiting the ghosts of a once hostile territory

After arriving at the Charles DeGaul Airport on Wednesday, Jackson and Lagerstrum made their way to the train station where they were met by two citizens of Saint Vougay, the daughter of a respected resident of Saint Vougay and her English speaking boyfriend. After a train ride of about an hour and a half, they arrived at the small village (about 200 residents) of Surdon where they stayed overnight in Destia Hermes's time share villa.

At Surdon Jackson was asked to attend a dedication of a monument in the village. The monument was located at the crash site of a B-17 which crashed landed there during WWII. The French partisans helped the American crew escape. In retaliation for helping the crew escape, the Germans purged the town of fourteen of its citizens. Later, only seven of the citizens returned alive.

After leaving Surdon, Jackson, along with some family members of George Wright, another crew member, who was the top gunner and engineer on *The Big Bitch*, consumed a day of traveling before they arrived at the revered site of the D-Day invasion on the Normandy Beaches. Jackson visited the St. James Brittany Cemetery where he was able to tilt his head and gaze down upon the graves of three of his fellow crew members who perished on that fateful day in 1942.

Later, Jackson was standing in the cemetery on Omaha Beach at the time taps was to be played as the American and French flags were to be lowered. Jackson was given the honor of lowering both flags, and of folding the American flag. "And, yes," exclaimed Jackson, "I saluted both flags." These two visits to the cemeteries was a very emotional time for 88 year old Jackson. His *heartstrings* were reacting to the memories of his mind; he choked-up, and moisture collected in his eyes. The cemeteries in France were unlike any Jackson had ever seen. They were flawlessly clean, and superbly manicured. Afterward, Jackson enjoyed an in depth tour of the monuments, museums and 60 year old fortifications. That afternoon, Jackson's party drove to Saint Vougay.

Jackson hears facts for the first time

At Saint Vougay, a small town of about 900, many citizens turned out to meet Jackson. Most of the store windows had been displaying large posters with Jackson's photograph and a brief explanation of his experiences—they knew he was coming. After stopping by the mayor's office, Jackson was met by over a hundred citizens who wanted to meet him. Many people brought delicious French dishes, and the celebration did not end until midnight.

The next morning Jackson honored a citizen's request to visit him at his home. The citizen, as a boy on his father's farm 65 years ago, had seen Jackson float down in his parachute from *The Big Bitch*. According to the man's story, it was obvious that the B-17 was shot-up. A parachute left the aircraft at approximately 10,000 feet. The body in the parachute hung limp, and swung helplessly around and around as the parachute descended. There was no life. There were no hands or arms reaching upward to the shroud lines to guide the parachute. As the parachute neared the ground, the canopy, which didn't seem to be fully opened, caught on the top of a tree and stopped.

Jackson spent two hours with the man while local television crews interrupted them for interviews. The old cart which the Germans confiscated to haul Jackson to the infirmary in was a cauliflower cart which belonged to the man's father.

Through out the next few days, several other local citizens approached Jackson telling him that they also had witnessed his fall from the sky. All of the witnesses corroborated the story. Most witnesses confessed that they could not tell if Jackson's body stopped before it hit the ground, or if the body hit the ground. To most of the observers, the flyer in the parachute was dead. Actually, it is the generally accepted belief, now, that when the parachute snagged the top of the tree, it *broke* Jackson's fall—thereby saving his life.

After the enlightened conversation with an actual witness of his decent from the B-17, Jackson visited a farm near the village. On the farm, Jackson was taken by complete surprise to see a whole wing of *The Big Bitch* (bullets holes and all) being used to enclose one complete end of the farmer's barn. Jackson was presented with a foot and a half piece of the wing to bring home. That piece also has some bullet holes in it that was punctured over 60 years ago by the guns of German fighters.

Later, Jackson participated in a local memorial dedicated to fallen troops of WWII. He participated in raising the America and French flags. An American small light airplane performed a one-plane flyover.

That evening ended with an array of delectable dishes at a dinner attended by 300 to 400 people in Saint Vougay. There were several speeches. Jackson spoke through an interpreter. Jackson was presented with a framed shadow box with a photograph of his crew, French and American flags and a Mae West life jacket.

A memorial to Jackson's crew

The last day that Jackson would spend in Saint Vougay and the nearby villages was a full day. The day began with a memorial and flowers at the Saint Vougay church, and afterward, a meeting with many veterans of the area. The afternoon began with a parade where Jackson rode in a WWII jeep. Many residents were wearing American military uniforms which they had garnered from the movie set of *Saving Private Ryan*.

After the parade, Jackson moved to the field where the memorial was to be erected. It was the crash site of *The Big Bitch*. A table was set up for Jackson to sign autographs. He signed on all kinds of items, including French underwear. A local radio station was broadcasting from the site, and the mayor of Saint Vougay presented Jackson with a gold book to sign which was to be enshrined in the mayor's office for eternity.

Flowers were placed at the memorial, and eight trees were planted, representing the eight members of Jackson's crew who lost their lives. A ninth tree will be planted soon for the pilot, John Bennett. After Jackson's death, a tree will be planted for him. The event was another very emotional period for Jackson, and again, his heart ached, and his eyes watered.

Aftermath

The next few days Jackson spent his time in Paris. He had the *grand tour*, and visited the renowned American hospital to which he was sent by the Germans. He looked out of the hospital window, and saw the Eiffel Tower just as he did as a wounded flyer over 60 years ago.

At the hospital, Jackson enjoyed a two hour lunch with Craig R. Stapleton (a cousin of First Lady Laura Bush), the American Ambassador to France, and three members of the Hospital Board.

Reflections

Jackson was treated like royalty—and he felt like royalty. He consumed a wide variety of foods, even duck, which before the trip he hated—but now he likes. He participated in two parades and signed many autographs. He met many people; and learned the facts about his drop from the B-17 on that fateful day in 1942. Jackson was given so many hugs and kisses, on both cheeks that in his words, "When the women kissed me on my cheeks, their tears were deposited on my checks to the extent that I thought my cheeks would never dry."

Jackson believes that the trip back to France finally brought some closure to his flashbacks of over 60 years ago. "The French people," recalls Jackson, "could not have been any nicer and respectful to me. They are great people." Of his experience, Jackson expressed, "I feel so fortunate that I was able to take this trip. It did so many things for me. I am very appreciative of such an opportunity." The French government is in the process of arranging for the order of the French Legion of Honor to be awarded to Jackson at a later date.

Jackson is an American patriot who objects vehemently to being called a war hero. But in this writer's opinion, he is just that—an American Hero.

Memorial to Jackson's crew near Saint Vougay at the crash site of the *The Big Bitch.*

Saint - Vougay

21 Octobre 1942
Crash d'un B 17 Américain
Abattu par les Allemands

21 Octobre 2007
Retour sur les lieux du dernier survivant

Samedi 20 et Dimanche 21 Octobre
de 10h00 à 19h00

"Nombreuses animations"
Exposition de véhicules et matériels 2° guerre
Reconstitution d'un camps US de 1944
Balade en Jeep
Crêpes et buvette sur place

Entrée Gratuite

Organisé par : amicale du 21 octobre 1942 et

The above poster is an invitation to join the ceremony to welcome the last survivor of the crash on Oct. 20 and 21 from 10am to 7pm. There will be activities and demonstrations of vehicles and items from WWII. There will be crepes and drinks.

Chapter 4

Lee Lamar
B-24 Pilot & POW

Final combat mission

On November 18, 1944, a B-24 Liberator took off from an air base near Spinazzola, Italy. Its mission was to bomb a German air base near Udine, Italy where enemy fighter aircraft were based. The ten man crew of the heavy bomber named, *Bottoms Up*, expected the mission to be a "milk run," because at the morning briefing it was reported that they expected fewer than usual anti-aircraft guns and fighters to resist the attack.

The copilot of the B-24 was Lt. Edgar (Lee) Lamar, a 23 year old farm boy from Faucett, Missouri. This would be Lamar's (called *Skippy* because he had skipped the first mission of the crew) 21st combat mission.

Over the target Lamar felt the release of the bombs and heard the bombardier call out "bomb bay doors coming shut." Before the bomb bay doors could be closed, "I felt the plane shudder, and knew that we had been hit badly," recalls Lamar. The bomber took a hit near the number one engine, and another one between the number two engine and the fuselage. The hydraulic and oxygen systems had been destroyed. Lamar later learned that a crew member of another bomber in the formation reported at the debriefing that "the last we saw them they were losing altitude fast with a hole in the left wing big enough to drive a Buick through."

As they neared the town of Pola, Italy, flak from enemy gun emplacements on the Brijuni islands off the coast destroyed the B-24's elevators, and almost immediately a piece of flak landed under Lamar's feet and destroyed the rudder pedals. Lamar looked at his pilot and said, "I think this is where we get off." All ten crew members bailed out. Lamar was next to the last out and felt he had only seven seconds between the time he left the aircraft and the time he and the aircraft hit the ground. The crippled bomber had been making a slow, wide death spiral to the ground. Soon the right wing hit the top of a tall Oak tree, and the B-24 careened into the ground. German soldiers arrived at the scene immediately, and occupied it for three days.

Lamar becomes a Prisoner of War
After Lamar landed, he rolled up his parachute and hid it behind a rock wall, covering it with dirt and leaves to conceal it. Lamar landed not far from his pilot, Randall Darden, and they both hid over night, but were captured by a German search party the next day. Four of the airmen were captured by the Germans; and six were eventually able to evade the Germans and return to allied territory with the aid of the local partisans. Lamar was ultimately transported to a POW facility, Stalag Luft I, near Barth, Germany. The Russian army reached Lamar's POW camp on April 30, 1945, and he returned home in June.

Lamar searches for information about the crash site
For over 60 years Lamar had been haunted by the memories of his experience. Thousands of times he had pictured in his mind's eye the location of his half buried parachute at the intersection of two old stone walls in the country side of what now is the country of Croatia. Events were replayed over and over in his mind; sadly, there seemed to be no closure.

Being adept with computers, Lamar researched processes *on line* in an unsuccessful attempt to find information about the crash site. Then, on September 17, 2006 (his wedding anniversary) bingo! Lamar hit the jackpot. He received an e-mail from a man named Luka Bekic. Bekic said he was an archeologist with the Croatian Restoration Institute, and that while "excavating a Roman Villa for a proposed pipeline, they had accidentally found an aircraft crash site nearby in a remote location near the village of Kravavici, Pula, Istria, Croatia." He continued with more information and finally stated, "Many things point out that our plane might have been yours." Bekic had researched the records and dates of downed aircraft in the area and was able to track Lamar through the internet. Over the next several months e-mails and invitations passed between Lamar and Bekic. Ron Wright, a member of the Commemorative Air Force (CAF), Heart of America Wing, was making arrangements with Lamar, also a member of the CAF, to make a trip to Croatia to revisit the crash site.

During a general meeting of the CAF at the New Century Air Center in Olathe, Kansas, Lamar excitedly announced his correspondence with Bekic. Dennis Okerstrom, a CAF member, and a professor at Park University, heard Lamar's announcement and decided that Lamar had a story to tell, maybe, even a documentary.

Okerstrom contacted Wright, and the planning and organizing for a trip to Lamar's crash site in Croatia began. Funding for the project was obtained from Park University, and on August 3, 2007 an entourage of 21 people left Kansas City for Croatia. Included in the group were Lee and Bonnie Lamar, their daughter and her entire family, Ron and Sharyl Wright, Dennis and Jeanette Okerstrom, eight Park students, and a two member film crew.

The group landed in Venice and the next day made their way across the Adriatic Sea to Pula, Croatia, a city with just over 62,000 residents. Pula, during WWII was spelled Pola, and was under Italian control. After WWII the city was part of Yugoslavia, before it became part of Croatia as it is today.

Lamar the celebrity

At Pula, the group was met by Bekic. After introductions all around, Lamar was transported to a Croatian air base in order to fulfill a prearranged appointment. The squadron consisted of about eight aging MIG 21s. Lamar walked down the small group of pilots as in a military review, shaking each one's hand as he passed. Also in the group were four elderly men in their eighties who had been partisans (underground resistance fighters against the Nazis). The partisans were responsible for saving many downed American pilots' lives. When Lamar met up with the partisans, emotions ran high for both parties. At the air base when Lamar shook hands with an aged partisan, the partisan placed his other hand on top of Lamar's and held it there for what seemed like a full minute. Through the interpreter, Bekic, Lamar thanked the partisans for what they did for him and his men during the war. The partisans returned their thanks, and the eyes of both Americans and Croatians moistened. A reception was held in Lamar's honor, and he was presented with a plaque.

Many newspapers and media carried Lamar's story. On the street, citizens approached him to shake his hand. Croatians offered to buy him wine, and even dinner. They thanked him from the depths of their hearts for his war-time service. Many times he found himself surrounded by curious, and grateful, people. According to Okerstrom, "Lamar was treated like a rock star."

The crash site

One morning, Lamar went searching for the spot by the wall where he had buried his parachute. He was sure he could recognize the location. After hacking his way through brush and high weeds, however, the location could not be found. Lamar was deeply disappointed. Lamar, for some reason, had focused concern over the years about his parachute. When asked why, Lamar said, "Well, it saved my life."

On the morning of August the 8th, Lamar traveled to the crash scene. During an interview with the older residents of the village of Krvavici, Bekic was told that, yes, they had seen a crash but no one had ever asked them about it. There were only very small scraps of the old B-24 visible. About three thousand small pieces had been excavated to date.

During the German occupation of the crash site, the engines and larger parts had been carried off, and thrown down the many deep sink holes (underground caves) which cover the fields; a practice that probably dated from ancient times. Some pieces of the aircraft were used by the local farmers to repair their dwellings. At one small farm, Lamar saw a bomb bay door from *Bottoms Up* being used to cover a farmer's wood pile. He also saw, according to villagers' eye witnesses' account, the tree that the bomber hit as it plunged to the ground. Lamar was silent, but obviously moved by the scene.

Parachute burial site

Lamar's group left the crash site and returned to the village where they were treated to a celebrity's welcome and a lavish meal. During the feast which consisted of some of the tasty local recipes, it was revealed that a 75 year old villager, Ivan Cetina, who was twelve years old at the time of Lamar's crash, had stated that his seven year old brother had found a parachute about seven days after the crash; and that he had gone back to the parachute and helped his seven year old brother carry it back home to their mother. Neither boy knew what it was. The mother immediately cut it up (she didn't want the Germans to know she had it) and made blouses for the girls in the family.

Ivan Cetina's younger brother was deceased, but his son, Ivan's nephew, led the group to the site. It wasn't long before the nephew pointed to a place on the ground where two old stone walls intersected. He explained that this was where the parachute was found.

Lamar gazed solemnly at the spot, and then walked back and forth in front of it. He walked about 20 feet down the other side of the wall where a small grove of trees once stood and stopped. He knelt down to look at the soil. It was loose and black, quite different from the other soils in the area. He related to Wright that this spot was probably the most meaningful of all to him "This is the place," recalled Lamar, "where I got on my knees, and asked for a little help." It was a very emotional moment for Lamar; and both he and Wright broke into tears. That moment 63 years ago for the 23 year old that was on his knees, became a kind of spiritual turning point in his life.

Lamar then pointed into the high brush in the other direction and remarked, "There should be a high rocky knoll up there a ways." He then walked about a hundred feet and found a spot which was solid rock. He looked around and said, "This is it." He was standing on the knoll on which he landed in his parachute in 1944.

Villagers recalled how they saw the B-24 making its wide turns as it fell from the sky. Eye witness accounts told of two smaller airplanes flying low over the site after the crash. Lamar, who had never mentioned the event before said, "Yes, there were two American P-51s who were evidently looking for me. I ran into a clearing and waved at them, but they didn't see me."

Lamar is officially honored

Stories and eye witness' accounts from villagers meshed with Lamar's memories; they confirmed the events. There was no question about it; Lamar had revisited the actual locations of those places that lingered in his mind for 63 years.

The next day Lamar visited Bekic's archeological office in a nearby village, where hundreds of small pieces of Lamar's B-24 were laid out. There were little scraps of metal, nuts and bolts, and even dismantled 50 caliber machine gun bullets. Bekic graciously allowed the visitors to take a few souvenirs.

On Friday Lamar was invited to the provincial capitol, Marciana, for an official welcoming ceremony. There were many who turned out to see Lamar receive a plaque presented by the mayor, and a number of other gifts, including a Rozenice, a popular folk instrument in Istria. Lamar presented the Mayor an American flag and displayed a Croatian ceremonial flag which Dr. Judy Vogelsang from the Honorary Council of Croatia, of Kansas City had sent along with him. Reporters from an array of newspapers, other media, photographers, villagers and even more partisans wanted to view, and to honor, the former American flyer.

Memorable results

Much of the Croatian media coverage emphasized two major aspects of Lamar's presence. One aspect was, of course, Lamar's return. The other aspect was that after sixty years of maintaining a low profile, partisans were coming out of the closet and identifying themselves. During WWII the partisans were part of a well organized, clandestine organization. They not only helped allied flyers escape, they sabotaged Nazi facilities and equipment and were responsible for the deaths of many of the enemy. If caught, they were shot.

Many of the partisans' neighbors felt that the partisans' activities resulted in hardship, punishment and death for innocent villagers in the hands of the occupying Germans. There were some bitter feelings. Consequently, after the war was over many partisans did not reveal their identities.

The partisans are now old men and women. A lot of water has passed under the bridge over 60 years; many of the citizens were dead, and not many cared anymore. Thus, the Croatian media was shocked by how many partisans were now identifying themselves because of the celebration of the return of a former American flyer and POW.

Lamar's trip back to the past was successful. Did the re-visitation of the events of 63 years ago finally bring a closure for Lamar? No one knows for certain. But it is hoped so. When asked how his trip was, Lamar replied, "I don't know how it could have been any better."

BELOW: Cetina (center) who was 12 years old in 1944.

BELOW: Bomb bay door used to cover the wood pile.

BELOW: B-24's oxygen tank used to feed farmer's cattle.

BELOW: Lamar, Sharyl and Ron Wright standing at the parachute burial site.

Chapter 5

Benedict (Ben) L. Lohman
Japanese Laborer

First published in The Best Times, a monthly publication of Aging Information & Action of Johnson County, Olathe, Kansas.

Background
Lohman, who was raised in Lansing, Kansas and attended the Kansas State Agricultural College (present day Kansas State University) for two years, came of age during the Great Depression. At age 19, because of poor job prospects, he became one of the two million men in America who were referred to as *hobos*. Even the seven months that Lohman illegally rode the rails, slept in *hobo jungles*, experienced hunger, bone-chilling cold nights, and some overnights in jails; he was not prepared for what he was to face a few years later when he was captured by the Japanese Imperial Army during the fall of Corregidor in 1942.

Peace-time Marine Corps
Lohman's adventure, or more appropriately defined as misadventure, began when he traveled to Kansas City, Missouri to join the United States Marine Corps in January of 1940. After completing boot camp in San Diego, California, Lohman was assigned to the Second Battalion, 4th Marine Regiment and sailed to

Shanghai, China where he spent twenty months as one of the 1,100 marines who protected American lives in the sector.

Because the Japanese were flexing their military muscles in Asia, foreign nations began removing their troops from Shanghai. The American contingent was the last to leave; and nine days before the Pearl Harbor attack the Fourth Marine Regiment's band played as the leathernecks marched down the streets to board a transport ship that would take them to Olongapoo, Philippines. Lohman, a Browning Automatic Rifleman, was in the group.

Since the Japanese forces had invaded Clark Field, Subic Bay and Olongapoo, General Douglas MacArthur ordered Lohman's 4th Marines to defend the small island of Corregidor. Bataan, which was separated by about three miles of water from Corregidor, surrendered on April 9, 1942. About a month later, on May 6th, after heavy bombardment, the marines on Corregidor were ordered to surrender, and 22 year old Lohman became a prisoner of war under the Japanese.

The first few weeks after surrender, Lohman was interned on the beach with ocean on one side and barbed wire on the other. They were given no food, water or medicine. After a few weeks, Lohman was sent by cattle boat to Bilabid Prison near Manila and later to Cabanatuan Prison Camps #1 and #2 where punishment was a firing squad. Again, there was no food or water, and Lohman was forced to eat monkey meat and snakes, if they could catch them. (He had eaten mule meat on Corregidor). Some men died for lack of medicine.

Slave Laborer

Eventually, Lohman boarded a troop ship and spent over twenty days in the hot, stinking hold before reaching Moji, Japan, where he was assigned as a slave laborer working in a ship yard.

Lohman's last forced stint as a slave laborer was in the copper mines in the Acknobe mountains, where he lived in a bamboo type structure and slept on a straw mat. After a breakfast of rice, six mornings a week, he would walk a three mile mountain path in his canvas thongs (the only shoes he had) to the copper mine where he descended 800 feet under ground to perform his work.

Before leaving to work in the mine in the morning, he would pack his lunch consisting of approximately two cups of cold rice in a small wooden box which the Japanese had issued to him. Lohman has that box to this day. Rice was the main staple of his diet. Sometimes he would have tea, beans, dried fish, three tiny pieces of some kind of bread or a small bowl of soup (mostly water).

He wore old worn out Japanese soldiers' uniforms which were already tattered and torn. He was allowed to bathe almost once a week in the same water in which the Japanese soldiers had bathed; but by then the water was filthy and of a thick soup-like consistency.

August 14, 1945 is a day that is indelibly etched in Lohman's mind; after three and a half years, he was finally free. On that glorious day, he was 26 years old and weighed 98 pounds.

Back in Kansas, Lohman became a prison officer, retiring from the Leavenworth Penitentiary as a guard and firearms instructor. Eighty-eight year old Ben Lohman lives with his wife, Frieda, in Fairway, Kansas and is very proud of his six children and ten grandchildren.

Japanese POWs

A Congressional Research Service Report for Congress by Gary K. Reynolds, an Information Research Specialist, wrote a paper entitled, *U.S. Prisoners of War and Civilian American Citizens Captured and Interned by Japan in World War II: The Issue of Compensation by Japan.* The paper, which was updated in November 2002, relates some facts about how captured Americans were treated by the Japanese.

Reynolds quotes Dr. Stenger, author of *American Prisoners of War in WWI, WWII and Korea,* as listing 93,941 U.S. personnel captured and interned by Germany, of whom 1% (1,121) died. The Japanese captured and interned 27,465 U.S. military personnel, of whom more than 40% (11,107) died.

Reynolds quotes statistics from Linda G. Holmes, *Unjust Enrichment: How Companies Built Postwar Fortunes Using*

American POWs, that evidence exists that POW camp commanders were given the latitude to kill all POWs if they felt they were a threat. The orders read in part, "annihilate them all, and not to leave any traces."

"Hell Ships"

Thousands of American POWs were shipped to the Philippines, Japan, China, Thailand and Korea as slave laborers, as in Lohman's case. The prisoners were crowded into the holds of ships which were ventilated poorly. Even though some of the trips would last for days, and weeks, the prisoners were given a minimum of food and water.

Many of these ships were owned by private companies. The ships did not carry identifying markings as a prison ship as prescribed by international law. Of the approximately 70 ships that transported prisoners, 21 were torpedoed. When a ship was sinking, the prisoners were left to fend for themselves. They were left in water to die, and some were even shot. According to Holmes, 17 of these ships were built, owned and operated by Mitsubishi, Kawasaki, Mitsui, and Yamashita Kisen.

When the American submarine U.S.S. *Snook* torpedoed the Japanese ship *Arisan Maru,* 1,800 U.S POWs were aboard, and only five survived. In another instance, the U.S.S. *Paddle* torpedoed the *Shinyo Maru* which was carrying 750 American POWs, of which only 82 survived. Of over 55,000 Allied prisoners shipped by sea, over 10,000 drowned.

Companies Using Slave Labor

Holmes estimates that about 50 firms can be documented as using American prisoners for slave labor. Further, that of the near 25,000 American slave laborers, over 4,000 died, mainly at the hands of their *employers*-- not the military. Even though the prisoners were promised some pay, it was rare that they ever received any. Some of the firms which used American slave laborers were: Mitsui, Mitsubishi, Nippon Steel, Showa, Denko and

Kawasaki Heavy Industries. Thus far, lawsuits for compensation have been unsuccessful.

Ben Lohman
Shanghai Light and Power Co.
Yangtze River Outpost 1941

BELOW: Ben and his wife, Frieda, attending a 2006 convention of "The Survivors of Bataan and Corregidor" organization.

BOOK II

Children Prisoners of War

Chapter 6

Betsy Herold Heimke

Teenage POW

While reading through *Prisoners of War,* Leathers Publishing Co., 2001, I came upon the story of Betsy Herold Heimke's experiences during WWII. I called Betsy, who resides in Overland Park, Kansas and asked her if I could tape an interview with her for the HOA's Newsletter. She granted an interview to me. So on a beautiful July day in 2004, I drove to Betsy's home where I met Betsy, and her husband who was a pilot during WWII.

I talked with Betsy for about three hours, and saw her mementos. She has some very interesting books in her library which chronicles the life of other women POWs, (women whom she had met), plus interesting literature on WWII Japan. We traded books. She loaned me two books with interesting accounts of women who lived in the hills of the Philippines during the Japanese occupation before becoming POWs, and in return, I loaned her my copy of *Flyboys*.

Betsy is a very sweet and gracious lady. More than once, while telling her story, her eyes were moist from tears, and she choked up. So did I. This is Betsy's story.

A new life

The morning of Monday, December 8, 1941 (the International Date Line placed the Philippines a day behind the United States) the Herolds began their normal day. Mr. Herold was ready to begin his day at the lumber mill, and Billy and Betsy were ready to leave for school. The announcement that the Empire of Japan had bombed Pearl Harbor came suddenly.

Ethel and Elmer Herold arrived in the Philippine Islands in 1922 in order to ply their trade as school teachers. Ethel taught English and history, and her husband, Elmer, taught science and mathematics.

Ethel and Elmer Herold were fond of the Philippines. They settled into a comfortable home, and soon added two children to their lives. Their first born was a boy whom they named Billy. Two years later Ethel conceived their second child, a girl, whom they named Betsy.

After Both Ethel and Elmer retired, Elmer went to work for a lumber company in the summer capitol of Baguio (**Bag** you o) on the island of Luzon, where Billy and Betsy had been born. Baguio, 150 miles from Manila, was a town nearly 6000 feet above sea level in the mountains. The climate was cool, and the surrounding landscape was dotted with pine trees, and provided a beautiful, picture-perfect scene of a Pacific paradise. Life for the Herolds was good.

Japan bombs the Philippines

The rest of the world, however, was not as serene as the Herold's small world. Only miles away, the nation of Japan began to stir the placid green-blue waters of the Pacific into a blood red roil. The implements and the men of war of the nation of the Rising Sun were spreading their deadly rays throughout Asia and the South Pacific.

Mrs. Herold proceeded to drive Billy and 12 year old Betsy to Brent School, a private Episcopal school on the island. According to Betsy, "The church school was an excellent school with an enrollment of fewer than one hundred."

As the regular morning school service ended and the candles were extinguished, the school children ran outside the chapel when they heard the loud roar of aircraft overhead. "We ran out and waved at the planes and cheered them on," remembers Betsy. "We knew our American planes were on their way to bomb Tokyo off the face of the earth in retaliation for Pearl Harbor." What the children didn't see, however, were the red circles of the rising sun on the underside of the aircrafts' wings. These airplanes with the rising sun (sometimes called fried rotten eggs) beneath their wings were about to create havoc on their island paradise.

A few hours later while Betsy was in class, she heard the sounds of aircraft again. As she looked, she heard bombs exploding and saw columns of black smoke. The windows in her school rattled. It was then that she realized that the airplanes were bombing Fort John Hay, the American army installation nearby which was established by the United States in 1903, and that the airplanes were Japanese.

When Betsy walked home from school that afternoon she saw two bomb craters about three feet from the back of her house. "My mother was going bananas," recalls Betsy, "and the servants were hysterical."

Mr. Herold decided that Betsy and Billy would be safer out of the house. Consequently, he took the children up a mountain trail to live with Mr. and Mrs. Kluge at one of his sawmills. Mr. Kluge worked for Mr. Herold as the superintendent of the sawmill.

Betsy and Billy stayed with the Kluges for a couple of weeks. All the while, they witnessed Japanese aircraft flying overhead constantly. "The overwhelming opinion of the adults," remembers Betsy, "was that a Japanese invasion would never happen. General MacArthur had enough men to protect them." (Later, the Kluges remained living in the hills as guerrillas. Mrs. Anna Kluge survived the war. Mr. Hermann Kluge did not).

In the meantime, Mrs. Herold did not want to spend Christmas without the children, so she drove to the Kluges and returned Betsy and Billy home. "When we returned," recalls Betsy, "our home was no longer a happy home." Strict black-out rules had been ordered. Blankets were hung over the windows. The telephone was ringing constantly with people asking the Herolds what they were going to do. Where were they going? The incessant bombing continued.

On December 24, 1941, the Japanese 9th Regiment occupied the Fort John Hay and the city. The beautiful Pacific paradise town of Baguio fell, according to Betsy, "without a whimper."

In the middle of the night on December the 27th, the doorbell rang at the Herold's household. When Mr. Herold opened the door, about 30 Japanese soldiers in battle-dress entered the home. Betsy remembered, "They looked fresh from battle. They had bushes and branches as camouflage sticking out from the netting on their helmets. They had bayonets on their rifles, and they just looked very mean."

Herold's are ordered from their home

The Herolds were ordered to stay in their home. They were going to be guarded; they should not run away. When asked if he had any guns, Mr. Herold lied, and said, no. They were ordered to report to Brent school the next morning to register. The Herolds were told to bring food, because the registration could possibly take three days.

The next morning the Herold family exited their home, and piled into their Studebaker; a Japanese soldier drove them to the Brent School. That was the last time they saw their comfortable island home, or their family car.

Upon arrival at the Brent school to begin the registration process, all sharp items were confiscated. The Japanese collected scissors, knives, razors, nail files and knitting needles.

Dinner that night for the Herolds consisted of taffy candy and a can of peaches which Mrs. Herold had thoughtfully put in her bag before leaving the house. Tragically, however, the food situation would deteriorate more profoundly in the future.

POWs at Fort John Hay

The next day all 500 of the Brent School registrants were ordered to walk to the former American army post at Fort John Hay. Betsy remembers the heat of the noon-day sun as the 500 civilians (including 17 pregnant women) trudged the five miles to the fort. Infants and children sobbed as their parents carried, and helped them make their way. Filipinos along the way were asking, "Americanos, what will happen to you?"

Upon reaching Fort John Hay, recalls Betsy, "We were all put in a dirty, bare, one-story barracks built for 40 soldiers. Everyone grabbed a cubical of floor space to call home." There was no electricity because of the destruction of the electrical generators by the Japanese bombs; there was no water supply, the toilets were running over, and there was no food available.

The Herolds were originally told that the registration process would take only 3 hours or three days. They began to realize, however, that going home in the near future was only a dream. The Herolds were prisoners of war.

Any money that was found on the captors was confiscated. They ate vegetables swept from the market floors and inferior rice which contained tiny stones. After their allotted two squares of toilet paper per day was used up, they used newspapers. Eventually, that would run out, too. The men in the work parties scavengered anything they could find to serve as cooking utensils, or garments.

The civilians knew that they must organize themselves in order to survive and to stave off dysentery and other diseases. Because Betsy's father had employed so many Philipinos, the Japanese chose him to be the liaison between the Japanese and the civilian prisoners. "My father just hated our Japanese captors," recalls Betsy. "They were so mean, and they wouldn't listen."

Finally, the Japanese let the prisoners set up school for the children. Books were smuggled over the fence of the compound, and Betsy was able to complete the 6th grade.

Twenty babies were born in the camp during the first six weeks of internment at Fort John Hay. In 1945, all twenty children were able to walk out of the camp alive.

The makeshift school which was established for the children in the prisoners' compound at Fort John Hay was forbidden by the Japanese to teach geography or history. The teachers defied the orders of their captors and taught the subjects anyway. To camouflage the grades in these subjects on the children's report card, however, the teachers listed them under *reading*.

There were 48 students, and 43 teachers. Because there were few books, missionaries and other adults taught what they knew. One day a Japanese truck drove into the camp courtyard, raised its gate and unloaded hundreds of small pieces of pink and yellow papers, which were old, used sales receipts from businesses. The children were wild with enthusiasm. They now had paper, because they could write on the backs of the receipts.

There were three students in Betsy's fifth grade class. To Betsy, "It was like having private tutors." Betsy completed the 5th, 6th, 7th, and 8th grade during her three years of internment. She was in the 9th grade when her confinement ended.

Transferred to Fort Holmes

After four months of internment at Camp Fort Hay, the 500 POWs were crowded onto Japanese military trucks and hauled to Camp Holmes, which was a few miles from the town of Baguio. The majority of the prisoners were Americans. The rest of the 500 civilians consisted of British, Canadian and Dutch business people, miners, teachers, a few retirees and children. Some of these people eventually died of sickness, starvation, torture, or simple old age.

Camp Holmes had been the Philippine Constabulary Post. It was a large installation which had been carved partially from the side of a mountain. Lingayen Bay, near which the invading Japanese forces landed, and later MacArthur's returning troops, could be seen from the site. The two story commanding officer's house was converted to a hospital. A small cottage next to the hospital was converted into the *baby house,* which sheltered the 20 babies among the group, and their mothers.

Because the Japanese forbid married couples to live together, the men and boys were housed in a two story barracks, and the women and girls were housed in another two story barracks. Single women occupied a single story barracks. Betsy slept on a door which her father had rigged to swing from the ceiling, thus, providing more floor space during the day.

The group of prisoners still wore the same clothing they had on their backs when they were forced from their homes. They would wear these same clothes for three years. They were told that the clothing on their backs belonged to the Japanese Imperial Army.

As the months passed, trousers had their legs cut off, and became shorts. The remaining pant legs were used to make potholders or other articles of clothing. Other pieces of clothing were used for cleaning rags and sanitary napkins. "We were the original recyclers," recalls Betsy. "A glass bottle with a lid and a tin can became a precious commodity. Wet diapers were many times reused before being washed. Our pencils had been sharpened down to an inch long, and very difficult to write with."

Camp life was drudgery. According to Betsy, "The single Red Cross shipment of food saved our lives. Mother made a can of spam last two days for the four of us. We got only 800 calories per day during the final days."

The greatest question on the prisoners' minds was, "Where was MacArthur? When are the Americans coming? The prisoners' minds were filled with disbelief, sadness and desperation when they heard that Bataan and Corregidor had fallen into the ruthless and greedy hands of the Japanese Empire. When they heard the thunderous explosions in the distance, they thought the Americans were returning to evacuate them.

They were aghast when they were told that California had been invaded, and that Japanese forces had made their way across the Mississippi River. They felt great sorrow to hear that Shirley Temple had died in child-birth.

"Our captors were an arrogant lot," remembers Betsy, "They enjoyed berating us as American citizens. One day a bus-load of Japanese school children came to see us. I felt like I was in a zoo being stared at."

When two prisoners successfully escaped from the camp, their three bunk mates, one with polio so badly that he couldn't stand, were taken out and strung-up by their thumbs and beaten with baseball bats, and almost tortured to death. One of the men was Betsy's teacher. She remembers sitting across from him and noticing that his thumbs looked like two little black sticks.

Betsy's mother, a very patriotic woman, and the other women in the camp pooled their skills to make an American flag. The white came from an ironing board cover, which determined its length, a blue napkin became the square, and the red was made from the caddie's uniforms at the old country club.

Betsy accumulated the bits of scraps left over from the ladies work, and made her own small American flag. One day when she was in the courtyard embroidering the stars, a Japanese guard leaned over her shoulder and uttered a kind of friendly comment, "Aw so, American flag." Betsy was so frightened that she ran into her barracks as fast as she could. Fortunately, the guard did not pursue her.

By the end of December 1944 the Rising Sun of the Empire of Japan was setting in the East. The Pacific Ocean was no longer theirs to roam; it was no longer an artery of transportation for supplies or transit. Saipan, Tinian and Guam, now in the hands of the United States, provided the U.S with air bases that placed our aircraft within striking distance of Japan, and the Philippines.

By mid December 1944, while inflicting a death toll of over 56,000 Japanese warriors, MacArthur was forcing his troops toward the beautiful island of Luzon.

Near the end of December, after being interned at Camp Holmes for two years and eight months, which marked her third year in captivity, Betsy's group were loaded on trucks for an unknown destination. As the trucks moved south, the POWs were aware of the heavy Japanese traffic moving north. General Yamashita needed Camp Holmes as a last defense against the invading Americans.

Old Bilibid Prison

Finally, the convoy stopped at the condemned Old Bilibid Prison near Manila. The two-story Bilibid Prison had been built by the Spaniards in 1898, and was surrounded by a 30 foot high electric fence. Betsy remembers, "Dad led us travel-weary four Herolds into the pitch-black cavernous two-story structure. We could hear rats scurrying about, and cockroaches crunch under out feet. This place was a dungeon. It stunk like a filthy sewer. We flopped onto wooden cots and upon awakening the next morning were covered with bed-bug bites."

There was never any refrigeration, or an ice box... Breakfast consisted of a small square of corn meal mush with little black weevils in it. Supper consisted of small pieces of a green celery-looking food called pachey, and a half of a camote, which was like a sweet potato; that was it...The Japanese usually ground up, what appeared to be navy beans. They mixed it with hot water and squeezed it to make their milk. They discarded the used, ground beans. The prisoners raided the garbage cans for the discarded leftovers. "We were down to about 600 calories a day," recalls Betsy, "and water was difficult to obtain. I don't think we could have lasted much longer than a month. Betsy was 15 years old.

The toilets consisted of a 20 foot slanted trough, which were flushed by tipping so that water in a can above would flow down the trough and into a ditch; which was always covered with large green flies. Water came from wells which had been dug next to the graves of former military POWs; and had to be boiled before use.

During Betsy's first days at Bilibid she witnessed B-24s drop their glistening bombs on the city of Manila. She was horrified when she saw a B-24 explode in the air, and two parachutes come down. According to Betsy, "Everyone cried."

Liberation

On the evening of February 3, 1945, Betsy's brother, Billy was ill. Betsy was sitting in her small cubical with others discussing how much they would like to have a small piece of bread. Suddenly, they heard a loud, grinding, crunching noise. "The noise got louder and louder until you could hardly hear yourself talk", recalls Betsy. "Suddenly, the Japanese opened fire on some tanks with bright red, orange streaks of fire. When the shooting started, My God, we knew the Americans had come back" The prisoner committee ordered all of the prisoners down stairs, and ordered them to sit tight.

When Billy and Betsy sneaked upstairs to steel some peanuts which mother had acquired, they looked out the window and saw eight Sherman tanks facing their compound. The Americans had no idea who, or what, was inside the Bilibid compound.

The next morning the Japanese notified the POWs that the Japanese authorities were no longer in control of them. "As the Japanese evacuated Bilibid," remembers Betsy, "they marched down the stairs with all of their canteens, rifles and equipment clanging. They looked at us so mean, with those little beady eyes, and the 456 of us just held our breath. Once outside in the street, the Japanese turned their rifles toward Bilibid as if they were going to fire at the POWs. Suddenly, Americans near the prison fired at the group of guards until there was no Japanese soldier left standing. Betsy's mother took out the homemade American flag and they sang the Star Spangled Banner and God Save the King. And they cried; they sobbed. Indeed, the fruits of their liberty were now close to the ground.

They were free, but they were still behind the prison walls. They didn't know what to do. They remained where they were, and listened as the noisy battle raged all through the night. Because of the intensity of the explosions of the battle, Betsy could see well enough to find her way to the bathroom outside. As she sat in the bathroom, she was overcome with excitement and joy when, through the semi-darkness, she heard an American male voice nearby say, "God Damit, Harvey, why aren't there any God Damn signs in this town?"... Betsy was afraid to yell out, or even make a sound.

That evening, as the American troops of the 37th Division were searching house to house; they opened a small window of Bilibid prison. The soldiers looked inside, saw Caucasians and said, "Hey, guys. how the hell do you get in this dammed place?" The response from inside was, "We have been wondering how the hell you get out of here for three years."

The POWs were as glad to see the soldiers as the soldiers were to see them. "And that's how we were liberated," recalls Betsy. "They were so up-beat, and cheerful, and happy, and handsome, and so big, compared to the shrimpy little Japanese guards. They gave candy, chewing gum, candy bars, and they gave the teenaged boys hands full of bullets, and for God's sake, a hand grenade to one boy." Later that day the soldiers brought some food to the newly liberated civilians.

That night Betsy and her father walked out into the compound and observed the scene. Manila was in flames. There were large billowing columns of smoke. Five and six story buildings were toppling to the ground like toys. The fire was inching closer and closer to the 456 ex-civilian prisoners, and the 811 military POWs, some of whom were bed ridden and veterans of Bataan and Corregidor, at Bilibid.

American army vehicles evacuated the two groups before the Japanese were able to blow-up the area with artillery. It was a slow, careful convoy that snaked its way through the front lines, the gun fire, the large blazing fires, and the smoke to deliver their precious, human cargo to Ang Tibay, an old shoe factory.

When the two groups arrived safely at the old two-story building, Betsy and her mother were able to visit with the military POWs. The military POWs were emaciated. Their skin which stretched thinly over their bones looked like leather...Their eyes were deeply sunken. They were as happy as the civilians were.

The American GIs strung bare light bulbs from the trees and bushes outside and set up a field kitchen. They fed the prisoners their first meal: dehydrated scrambled eggs and coffee with real sugar and canned milk. It was a very exciting and festive time for Betsy and her family.

Parked in the area was an army truck with various radio equipment packed in the back. And typical of GIs, the radio was blaring with music from stateside… The music stopped and the announcer said, "In the Pacific Theatre we have just leaned that several thousand civilian POWs have just been liberated from Manila. I will now sign off. This is San Francisco, The United States of America." "A great sense of Euphoria, joy, ecstasy overwhelmed everyone, and an abundance of tears, and we all hugged each other," remembers Betsy. "Hey! We all shouted. We are actually Free! Yippee! Free!"

Because the Japanese were attempting to annihilate the group at Ang Tibay, they were convoyed back to the Bilibid Prison. It was different this time, however, because Betsy and her family were free; and they had food and water. However, during the month that they were there, they faced constant shelling from the Japanese. It was a miracle that no one was killed by shrapnel. Some of the teen age boys from the camp joined with the American GIs to help load the large guns which retaliated against the Japanese fire. When Manila fell near the end of February, Betsy and her mother were air lifted to Leyte by a C-47 (in fact, Betsy flew in the copilot's seat) where they slept in an army tent and gorged themselves with the delicious army food.

Back to the USA

When Betsy, her mother and father (Billy had returned to the states earlier), sailed under the Golden Gate Bridge in San Francisco, according to Betsy, "There was not a dry eye on the deck."

After a brief stay with friends in California, Betsy and her parents traveled to Missoula, Montana where Billy had already enrolled in high school. In 1946 Ethel and Elmer Herold returned to Baguio to run the mining company. Ethel and Elmer felt a strong bond with the Philipinos who had helped them survive during the war. They remained there for fifteen years.

Billy and Betsy remained in the United States. When Betsy was a senior in nurse's training at Northwestern University, she married Karl Heimke, whom she had met on a blind date and was a senior in law school at the University of Wisconsin. Karl had been a pilot in USAAF during the war. After living in several cities Betsy and Karl eventually settled in Overland Park, Kansas. Betsy married and was blessed with four children, and five grandchildren.

Among Betsy's treasured mementoes are: The shorts she wore for over three years which were made from her girl scout skirt, a small doll with clothes which she knitted while in camp, and the small American flag which she made from scraps. This flag commands an honorable and prestigious place on her living room wall.

BELOW LEFT: The location. BELOW RIGHT; Betsy and her family in front of their home in Baguio before becoming Prisoners of War.

TOP RIGHT: Betsy's parents after liberation. Both had gained ten pounds at the time of the picture. **BELOW LEFT**: Betsy standing in a Red Cross line at Bilibid. **BELOW RIGHT**: Betsy's home on Luzon in 1948. Only the chimney standing.

Chapter 7

Frank Saunders, Jr.
Child Prisoner of War

Background

Salem, Massachusetts is probably better known for its colonial witch trials than it is for its once thriving textile mills. By 1939, however, with the textile industry declining in the northeast, and the ever present economic cloud of the Great Depression over most Americans' heads -- times were tough. Frank Saunders, a mechanic repairing looms and other equipment in a Salem textile factory, could hardly make ends meet. Saunders wife, Emma, worked as a police woman supervising women prisoners in order to help provide for the family.

In 1939 Saunders discovered an advertisement in a local newspaper recruiting textile workers to go to work in the Philippine Islands. The United States was attempting to help the Philippines prepare for its future independence. Thus, the United States was willing to pay good wages, and transportation, to place people in positions to train the Philippine workers the skills they would need when they became self-sufficient. It sounded like a good way out. The family decided to go to Manila. That decision was responsible for changing the Saunders' lives forever.

In 1939 Frank and Emma and their three children Frank, Jr. age 8, Norma age 13 and Dorothy age 18 began their exciting adventure. It was exciting for the family to cross the United States by train all the way to the sunny shores of San Diego, California. In San Diego the Saunders family boarded the *SS President Cleveland* for the voyage to the Philippines. Before reaching the Philippines, the ship stopped in Hawaii for three days before proceeding. Young Frank, as an eight year old boy, couldn't have been more excited. He still recalls that excitement today. Not many boys could take their first train ride, see the hills, plains and mountains of America; and board their first ocean liner for the romantic tropical islands in the Pacific.

The good life

Upon arriving in Manila, the Saunders moved into a new home. It was not a huge home, but it had three bedrooms and a large porch. It was a nicer home than they ever expected to live in had they stayed in Salem. Mrs. Saunders no longer had to work outside the home, and even had a 16 year old Filipino houseboy whom they called Johnny.

Mr. Saunders made good money working for the National Textile Company, and the whole family was happy with their new environment. "We were living high on the hog," recalls Frank Saunders, Jr. Young Saunders attended the school established for the military children.

A year after arriving in Manila, 19 year old Dorothy married US Army Captain Riley Bass. Bass was a bright and up-coming star who had graduated second in his class at West Point three years earlier. In 1940, soon after their marriage, the US Army ordered the new Mrs. Bass (Dorothy) back to the United States.

The serene life of the Saunders would soon begin to shatter. While eating breakfast on the morning of December 7, 1941 the Saunders' quiet and peaceful morning was disrupted by the droning of aircraft engines. At first they thought that the Americans at nearby Clark Field were engaged in another practice exercise. But when they looked up and saw the solid red ball which represented the rising sun of the Imperial Japanese Empire on the wings of the aircraft, and the bombs being dropped on Manila which was only about six miles from their home, they knew that their life was about to change.

Japanese invasion

Ten hours after the Japanese attack on Pearl Harbor, Japanese aircraft rained their bombs on American air bases in Manila. They destroyed General MacArthur's small air force while it was still on the ground. Only nineteen days after the surprise bombing of Manila, Manila was declared an "open city" (there would be no resistance) and the Japanese took control of Manila and the US Navy base at Cavite. On January 3, 1942, not quite a month after the initial bombing, the Japanese soldiers, with bayonets on their rifles, invaded the privacy of the Saunders' home by kicking in the door.

The soldiers took all items of value. Later, they returned and forced Mr. Saunders to leave with them. Later that night a soldier returned and demanded a blanket. Mrs. Saunders and the two children were terrified that Mr. Saunders had been killed, and that the blanket was going to be used to wrap his body. Their fears were relieved the next morning when Mr. Saunders returned home still quite alive. The employees of the textile factory had removed several parts from the textile machines and threw them in a river in order to render the machines incapable of functioning. The soldiers had taken Mr. Saunders away to have him fix the equipment. When they found that he didn't have the parts, they returned him unharmed.

Any joy left in the Saunders family was soon shattered the next morning when they and about 400 other civilians were ordered to evacuate their homes immediately. They were loaded aboard crowded trucks with only the clothes on their backs. The trucks unloaded the civilians at a movie theater in Manila. For three days the civilians sat cramped in the theater chairs wondering what was going to happen to them. The civilians, now prisoners, lined up three times a day to be fed poor rice, *lagau*, which had been cooked so much with water that the grain was no longer part of it. At the end of the third day, the prisoners were again ordered to board trucks and were transported to Sánto Tomas University.

Sánto Tomas Internment Camp

Sánto Tomas was an agricultural college. The main building with classrooms was five-stories. The men and the women were separated. Young Saunders and his father slept on the fourth floor. At first, they slept on the concrete floors of the small, crowded, unbearably hot classrooms. The Red Cross was eventually able to provide cots, beds and bedding for the prisoners. The university was bulging at the seams with hundreds of prisoners, and became an official internment camp.

The prisoners were fed three meals a day consisting of fish, sometimes meat, lagau and vegetables. The discipline was not real strict at first, but all prisoners were expected to be in bed by 9 PM. Fortunately, Frank Sr. had hidden money in his shoe and, with the aid of their houseboy, Johnny, was able to supplement their diet. One day a week Frank Sr. would leave a note with a guard which Johnny picked up. A week later when Johnny delivered the package, he would receive a package with money in it.

Referring to the prisoners and the guards during these early stages of internment, the situation was foreign to both the guards and the prisoners. Saunders recalls that, "We didn't know how to treat one another." It wasn't long before the prisoners began to organize their lives.

There were varied professional skills among the conglomerate of prisoners. Schools were established, and taught by the prisoners. Saunders learned to play golf, which he enjoyed the rest of his life. The prisoners stood roll-call every morning and evening. The prisoners hesitated to escape (plus, there was no where to go) because the Japanese would punish other prisoners remaining in the camp. Later during the war, this punishment very well could be death.

Los Baños Internment Camp

The conditions at the Sánto Tomas Internment Camp were crowded and unbearably hot. There was little privacy, especially for families. When a group of prisoners pleaded with the Japanese to let them build some barracks-style buildings at another location on good farm land formerly owned by the university, about 40 miles away, Saunders was among the prisoners who helped build them. "The Japanese," recalls Saunders, "felt they had to get us out of there before we all died."

Actually, Japanese construction crews built about 30 barracks buildings in an open field. The buildings were constructed with wood frames, sawali sidings (thinly split bamboo woven to form mats) and nipa roofs (a plant with wide leaves). Some of the buildings had dirt floors, a few concrete floors, and a few bamboo floors. The buildings were 150 feet long, 40 feet wide, and housed between 75 and 100 prisoners. Families set up their own areas within the building. The buildings were poorly constructed and many of them fell apart as time went by.

The camp had two barbed wire fences, about 12 feet apart which encircled the camp. Ten guard towers with machine gun armed Japanese soldiers lined the fences. Japanese forces within the vicinity of the camp at several locations numbered over 9,000 troops by then. The Japanese units were heavily armed with small weapons and large guns.

The barracks living at their new home, called the Los Baños Internment Camp, with its private entrance and plot for gardening suited the Saunders much better. The Saunders were able to plant some vegetable seeds which they had received from Johnny. However, as the war progressed, the garden plots disappeared as the Japanese built more and more housing for prisoners.

The civilian prisoners were told early in captivity by Japanese diplomat, Mr. Kodaki, that as long as the war went well for the Japanese Empire the prisoners would be treated magnanimously. The prisoners were fed three meals a day at first, but as the war wore on, meals were reduced to two a day. At meal time the prisoners would stand in long lines. Each carried a card that was punched by a Japanese guard, so that no one could get in the line again for seconds.

Breakfast consisted of rice and coffee. The evening meal consisted of a ladle of rice and a ladle of stew. The stew had a little talinum in it. Talinum was called New England spinach by the prisoners, and when cooked tasted slimy and metallic. Meat was rare. Near the end of the war the prisoners tried to survive on an inadequate amount of unhusked rice. During the last months of the war some prisoners were reduced to eating weeds, vines, salamanders, and slugs or grubs. Eventually, dogs and cats, if they could be found, and rats were cooked. There were deaths every day. About seventy percent of the prisoners suffered from beriberi, dysentery and malnutrition. It was difficult to assess the prisoner population because of death and others coming and going. But there were well over 2,000 prisoners in the camp. Interned within the barbed wire compound were Protestant missionaries and their families, Catholic nuns, priests, doctors, engineers, other professionals and their families, and a few wives and children of American servicemen.

Saunders learns to barter

Saunders was not a large boy. In fact, and especially because of his diet, he was small. His physical size, along with his early teen years, however, served him well. Many times Saunders would crawl under the barbed wire fences and sneak into some of the small Filipino villages and barter for food. He would take whatever he had, and trade it to someone who had something he didn't have. A pair of shoes was a good item of barter, and sometimes would bring a chicken. Saunders would weave mats and barter with the other prisoners or villagers. He would help build cookhouses and other additions for barter. Saunders collected all kinds of items. "I got to be pretty good at bartering and setting up exchanges," remembers Saunders. "I got to the point that I could arrange about anything. I was a 13 year old boy going on 45."

Even though the Japanese threatened to shoot anyone who was leaving the camp, or coming in, Saunders roamed all over the countryside between roll calls. He brought back fruits and other staples to feed his very ill mother. According to Saunders, "I, and other people, believe that by sneaking around bartering, and bringing food home to mother was the only thing that kept her alive.

Camp administration

The prisoners created their own Prisoners Administration Committee (PAC). The seven members helped keep discipline and order within their own ranks. They negotiated with the Japanese for food, and the opportunity to barter for food. The PAC operated with the consent of the Japanese.

The PAC tried to control rumors, and even assigned their people to the assorted Japanese work details. Saunders was assigned to the burial detail, and spent back breaking hours working in the tropical heat.

The early commandant of the Los Baños Camp was a Japanese colonel named Urabi. Even though the war was turning sour for Japan, Urabi did not punish the internees. Urabi was not known as a tormentor, and even allowed the internees to obtain food, or bring food into the camp.

In June of 1944, however, Major Iwanaka became camp commandant, and conditions very quickly changed. Iwanaka is described as a man in his fifties who really didn't want to be bothered by the whole thing. He moved about in his pajamas, tended his garden, and left most decisions to his administrator of finance and supply, Warrant Officer Konishi.

Konishi had been in the Philippines for only a few years. Much of that time he had been in hospitals suffering from tuberculosis. The 5' 7" Konishi was reputed to have an intense hatred for the white race. He has been described by some of the prisoners as sadistic, ferocious, ignorant, brutal and a filthy-bodied little Jap.

Konishi eventually cut the per day rice ration per prisoner down to 150 grams. He destroyed the camp's gardens, and did not allow any food from the villages to be bartered for by the prisoners. The prisoners' health became worse. Prisoners were dying of starvation and disease.

By 1944 the Empire of Japan was on the defensive. The internees never really knew what was going on in the war. They were able to follow some of the events through hidden radios. Sometimes, a local Filipino would fill them in with a shred of news. They realized something was going on when American money and cigarettes showed up with some of the Filipinos who traded with the Japanese.

The prisoners also noticed American aircraft flying overhead, low enough that they could see the Americans. After awhile, the Japanese forbid the prisoners to look up at the aircraft, and tried to herd them inside so they couldn't look up.

The liberation of Los Baños

By January 1945 the American forces were in the Philippines. General Douglas MacArthur had the liberation of all of the prisoners in the Philippines high on his priority list. The Americans put together information on the defenses of Los Baños, which was 25 miles behind the Japanese lines, by secretly talking with local Filipinos and taking aerial photographs of the camp.

By late January and early February, American forces liberated about 1,800 internees and POWs from two camps, plus 3,700 from Sánto Thomas University.

On the morning of February 23, 1945 the internees were forming for roll call. When the sick and weary prisoners turned the eyes toward the drone of engines in the sky, they counted nine airplanes. The airplanes were American C-47s; and they were loaded with paratroopers from the US 11th Airborne Division. Soon the sky was filled with parachutes. Some prisoners were elated that the Americans were dropping food for them. As the parachutes came closer in view, the prisoners realized that men were in the parachutes. They couldn't believe it. They were being liberated.

The mortar guns were firing, the ground was shaking, and the soldiers rushed the camp. The battle lasted for about twenty minutes. When it was over, 243 Japanese guards had been killed or had run for their lives. None of the prisoners, or any of the invading force was killed.

The liberators were hugged and kissed by the prisoners. The whole camp was cheering. Some were praying, and some were crying. "I saw these big tank-like things moving toward our camp," remembers Saunders. "They just came through the fences and bamboo. They drove right into a pond and kept coming. I couldn't understand why they were driving into the water." What Saunders saw was the army's amphibious "amtracks" which very shortly were to haul him away from Los Baños. Some 130 of the internees were too weak to walk to the military vehicles, and had to be carried by the soldiers.

Evidently, the raid on the camp could not have come too soon. According to General MacArthur's information, all of the prisoners at Los Baños were to be shot and killed as they stood in a group at roll call on the 23rd, the morning of the attack.

The amtracks took the freed prisoners to Mamatid which was behind American lines. They were then loaded on 21 trucks and 18 ambulances and transported to New Bilibid Prison in the city of Muntinlupa, about 15 miles away.

Going home

Saunders and his family stayed in the New Bilibid Prison compound for several weeks before they were evacuated to the United States. Conditions were much better, however, and the former internees had plenty, at last, to eat. In fact, a problem arose because the internees had too much to eat. The problem was consistent with liberated persons from prison camps all over the world. Upon liberation, former prisoners were so starved that they stuffed themselves and became sick. The military tried to limit the food until the former internees were able to begin a more normal food intake. Saunders loved the food, especially the chocolate candy bars.

All former internees had to undergo physical examinations before they were released. Frank Saunders, Sr. was pronounced to be in good health. Even though young Saunders contacted malaria twice, had cavities in every tooth, and was undernourished, he was considered in decent health. Mrs. Saunders was still ill, but considered in "fair" health.

The oldest Saunders of the three Saunders' children, Norma, who had married army officer Riley Bass, and then was ordered to the United States, was living in Kansas City, Kansas. The Red Cross notified Norma of their release and Saunders Sr. decided to locate in the vicinity. The family learned that Riley Bass was captured by the Japanese in 1942 and became part of the Bataan Death March. The Japanese captivity reduced the once vibrant, intelligent Bass to a walking ghost. He was never able to recover. When Bass was about 70 years old, Saunders saw him at a public event, where Bass was selling cold beverages from a pack strapped to his back. "It was one of the saddest things I ever saw," recalls Saunders.

Saunders sailed from the Philippines on the *USS Admiral E. W. Eberle* and stepped upon American soil in May. Mrs. Saunders, who went from 148 pounds down to 76 pounds, passed away in June. Frank Saunders Sr. settled in Atchison, Kansas where he worked as a manager in a manufacturing company. He lived to be 101 years old.

Aftermath

Saunders lived with his sister Dorothy and attended eighth grade at Northwest Junior High School in Kansas City, Kansas. Known as a "problem child", he moved to Atchison to live with his father. The year before he graduated from Ottawa University, he married Yynona Piersol, to whom he has been married all of his life. They produced three children. After college and marriage, Saunders was drafted into the US Army, and was trained as a teletype operator.

Saunders became a senior partner in the law firm, Saunders, Austin, Brown & Enochs, which he established. It became the largest law firm in the state of Kansas. He was active in city, county and state civic organizations before retiring in 2000. In 1972 Saunders revisited Johnny in the Philippines. It was an emotional experience, even though it was too dangerous, at the time, to revisit some of the places which are indelibly etched upon his memory.

The Saunders family was not only touched by war, they were kicked in the stomach by it.

BELOW: Second and third from left, Norma and young Saunders pose with their liberators of the 11th Airborne Division at New Bilibid Internment Camp a month after leaving Los Baños.

BELOW: Internees being fed at New Bilibid.

BELOW: Saunders as a 13 year old junior high school student in Kansas City, Kansas in 1945.

BELOW: Sánto Tomas was liberated 20 days before Los Sañtos. This photo from the March 5, 1945 issue of *Life Magazine* Shows two civilians after their liberation.

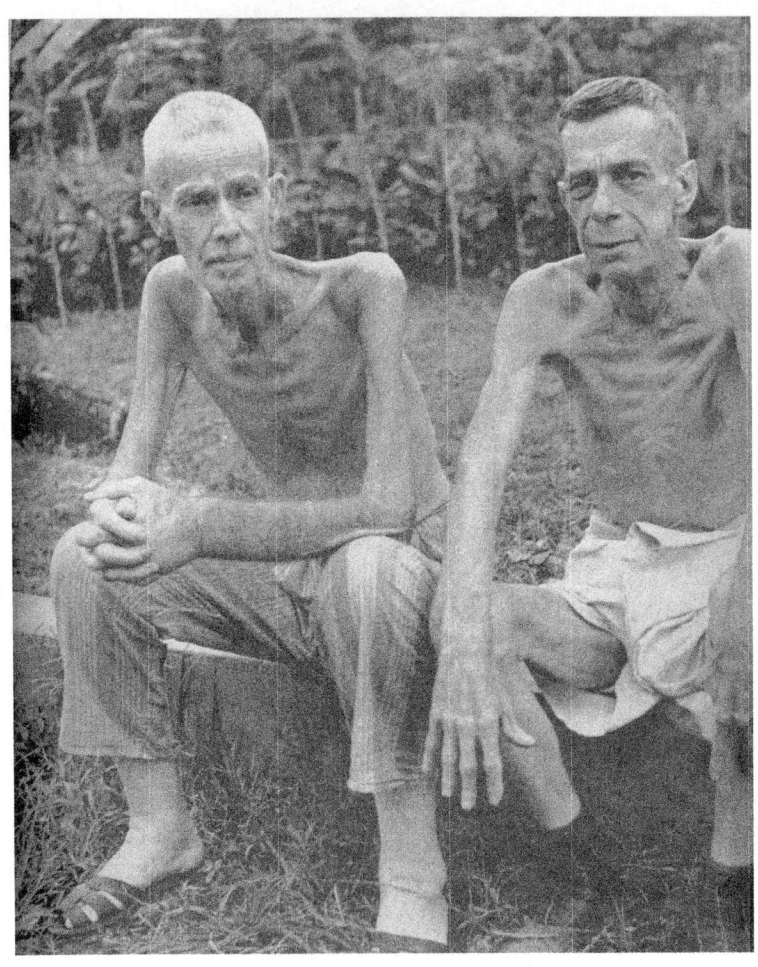

BOOK III

Children Under Fire

Chapter 9

Dorinda Nicholson
Pearl Harbor Attack

The following story is a summary of the experiences of Dorinda Makanaōnlani Nicholson who was living in Hawaii during the Japanese attack on Pearl Harbor. She was gracious enough to permit me to tell her story which she has recounted in her published book, *Pearl Harbor Child*, First Revised Edition, Woodson House Publishing, K. C., MO, 2001. All of the photographs which appear in this story are from Nicholson's files.

The surprise
Six year old Dorinda lived in the tranquil community of Pearl City, Hawaii on the island of Oahu. Her family's home was located on the Pearl City Peninsula, a small strip of land surrounded on three sides by Pearl Harbor.

Dorinda lived a contented life with her mother, a local Hawaiian, who worked in the offices of Pan American Airways; her father, a Caucasian, who worked in the post office; her younger brother; and her dog, Hula girl. The Pearl City community was made up of an interesting variety of citizens.

There were fishermen, merchants, storekeepers, military officers and rice farmers. Many of the Americans in Pearl City would not have to look too far back in their history to prove their Japanese ancestry. There was a small hotel, a yacht club, and the Pan American Clipper base. The moored clipper ships provided a backdrop for the many times that Dorinda and her friends dropped their fishing nets into the bay to catch crabs.

On Sunday, December 7, 1941, first grader Dorinda was sitting down to a breakfast of Portugese sausage, rice, eggs and papaya fruit. Beautiful music from the big console-type radio in the living room drifted into the kitchen. It was another delightful morning in Hawaii.

The peaceful scene was suddenly destroyed by the sounds of low flying airplanes which streaked directly over Dorinda's house. There were loud explosions; more airplanes, and then more explosions. When Dorinda's father jumped up from the table to dash outside, Dorinda was right on his heels.

The Japanese airplanes were so low that one could see the orange and red symbols of the rising sun painted on their wings. Dorinda remembers seeing the faces of the pilots with their goggles over their eyes. The noise of the airplanes' machine guns was drowned out by the roar of the aircrafts' engines.

As they looked around, they discovered that the kitchen of their house was on fire, part of the roof was gone, and the front door of their neighbor's house had been shot from its hinges.

Dorinda's father ordered the family into their 1939 Ford sedan so they could escape the harbor. Due to the emergency needs of the streets and roads, the military ordered all civilian cars off the streets in order to mobilize the military. The car radio was screamingly announcing the attack, and ordering all military and medical personnel to report to their quarters or the hospitals. Dorinda's father, determined to hide his family, found another route to a vantage point by the harbor. According to Dorinda, "…what we saw will never be forgotten."

The shock

From her vantage point, the burning oil in the water made it look as if all the water was on fire. It was obvious that men had been killed, and were still dying. When Dorinda's father decided to return home, he was ordered by military police to go somewhere else where it was safe. Hawaii was under martial law, and the military was now in control.

Dorinda's father finally steered the black ford into a sugar cane field nearby, and parked among the stalks. Soon they were joined by other local residents and their families who were also looking for a safe place to go. As time passed, some of the younger children began to cry. Some of them were hungry.

The adults knew little about the attack. They could only come up with guesses to their own questions. Would the Japanese aircraft return again to bomb? Will they return many times? Were all islands being attacked? Have the Japanese ground forces landed yet? Will they? Would they ever be able to return to their homes again?

As darkness approached the group in the cane fields, the carnage in the harbor continued. Explosions continued to pierce the smoke filled air as more ammunition storage areas were reached by fire, and plumes of fire reached upward toward the sky.

Among the pungent odors in the air from gas, oil, munitions and fire, the families began to bed-down for the night in the cane fields. Before that could happen, however, the military police arrived in the cane fields. The military told them they could not return to their homes, and instead led them to a recreation hall at a sugar mill about ten miles away.

The recreation hall contained a small soup kitchen and one bathroom. The group of about 100 men, women and children slept on the hard floors. The use of telephones was prohibited.

The silence of the night was suddenly shattered by gun fire. Red streaks were seen flashing over the harbor. Many of the group believed that the Japanese invasion had begun. Just as suddenly, the firing stopped. People wondered if the Japanese soldiers were ashore. Dorinda describes the atmosphere for the rest of the night in her book, *Pearl Harbor Child:*

"The remainder of the night was spent in fear, wondering what the latest exchange of gun fire meant. The radio was silent, so we had no information. The phones were still restricted to official military use, so we couldn't call anyone to let them know we were safely out of the harbor. There was nothing to do but huddle together in the dark, draw our families close to us, wait for morning, and quietly ponder the unforgettable events of December 7, 1941."

By the time Dorinda and her family, mired in confusion and uncertainty, tried to settle in that night, Americans everywhere had heard the news. America (and the rest of the world) was in shock. The United States was rudely shaken from its long sleep, and complacency, by the strong hands of war.

Most Americans never saw it coming. Ironically, it was the radio signals of the beautiful music Dorinda was listening to on that peaceful Sunday morning that helped guide the attacking Japanese aircraft to Pearl Harbor. The day was described by President Franklin D. Roosevelt as, "...a date that will live in infamy." History has proven him correct. Many Americans related to the story of a young sailor who was in the attack, and after learning that the aircraft were Japanese, allegedly said, "I didn't even know they were mad at us."

Damage assessment

The next morning, Dorinda and the other evacuees awakened from a fitful sleep in the sugar mill. Those who worked left the mill to go to their jobs. Dorinda's father went to Honolulu to his government post office job. The rest of the families remained in the mill and huddled around the radios listening to whatever news they could find. When the spouses returned to the mill after work, they were able to bring back bits and pieces of news. The *Honolulu Star Bulletin,* even though heavily censored, provided some news of the attack.

As the days passed, figures on the losses on that fateful morning began to take shape.
- Of the eight battleships in the harbor, all were damaged. Five of them were sunk, sinking or totally damaged. *The USS Arizona* lost 1,177 men, most of whom are entombed in the ship; and the *USS Utah* has 58 men entombed on board.
- Three cruisers, three destroyers and a seaplane tender were severely damaged.
- Ninety two U.S. Navy aircraft were lost, 31 damaged.
- Seventy seven U.S. Army aircraft lost, and 128 damaged.
- Over 2,400 men were killed, and 2,000 wounded. (Twenty nine Japanese aircraft were lost.)

It was discovered that the sudden firing late on the day of the raid was from the American military. A group of navy fighters known as the "Fighting Six" from the aircraft carrier *USS Enterprise* were trying to land on Oahu. American gunners at Pearl Harbor, still nervous from the Japanese surprise attack, fired on the American fighters with all they had. That friendly fire accounted for the loss of five of the American airplanes, and three pilots. One of the fighters crashed into a small hotel just one block from Dorinda's house, and the pilot was killed. American anti-aircraft fire, which fell on Honolulu, caused extensive damage, along with the killing of three civilians in a car about eight miles from Pearl Harbor.

After the attack
After five days of sleeping on the hard floors of the sugar mill, the evacuees were allowed to return to their homes. Dorinda was ecstatic because she was worried about her dog, Hula Girl. "I could hardly wait," recalls Dorinda.

Upon arriving at their home, Dorinda's family was pleased to see that their house was still there. Before the family was out of the car, Dorinda was calling for Hula Girl. When Hula Girl did not appear, Dorinda was heart broken. She walked the streets calling for her dog until darkness fell. She began to believe that her beloved pet had been killed during the attack; or worse yet, wounded, and crawled off somewhere to die.

As Dorinda lay in her own soft bed and clean sheets, her sadness did not allow her to appreciate the elation of being home again. Suddenly, during the silence, she thought she heard a weak whimpering sound. She jumped up and looked under her bed. But, she saw nothing. Once again in bed, she thought she heard the whimper again. She grabbed a flash light, and she and her father went outside. They looked under the house which was built about eight inches off the ground on stilts. The flashlight beam highlighted Hula Girl. Although very weak, she was alive. Hula Girl was given her name because when she wagged her tail, her hips would move as if she was doing the hula. After a few days of tender, loving care, Hula Girl was back in action.

The schools were closed since the attack, and did not reopen until February of 1942. Most of them had been converted into hospitals.

During those months, Dorinda found plenty of time to be with her friends and, of course, Hula Girl. Her mother was home too, because her job at Pan American had been put on hold. Because of rumors of poison being in the water, her mother saw to it that their bath tub was constantly full of water.

The children created a game out of the shrapnel and used bullet casings scattered about, by seeing who could collect the most. Dorinda's father consistently found blackened streaks and bullets in the walls of their kitchen. To this day, Dorinda has the Japanese bullet which her father dug out of the wall above their telephone.

Because much of Hawaii's food was imported, the residents became fearful that supply ships might be cut off from arriving. Long lines formed at the groceries stores. Many people attempted to hoard food, which only made the problem worse. Finally, only so many people were allowed in the stores at a time.

Soon after the attack, long lines of people filled the steamships to capacity in an attempt to leave the islands. But the government wanted even more people to leave the islands because there would be fewer mouths to feed, and fewer civilians to protect in case the Japanese returned. Consequently, the government ordered all civilians who did not have a job which contributed to the war effort to leave, including the wives and children of the military. Residents could take their choice. Since the islands were home to Dorinda's mother, and her father worked for the post office, they were allowed to stay. But Dorinda saw many of her friends leave the islands.

Military law dictated that everyone over six years old be fingerprinted and carry an identification card. The card served a dual purpose. Not only was it a method by which saboteurs would be kept out, it also served as a method of identifying those injured or killed in further attacks or invasions.

Hawaii digs in for defense

The military and the people in Hawaii always lived with the fear in the back of their minds that the Japanese were not finished with their attacks on the islands. The beautiful island of Oahu was transformed from an island paradise and vacation mecca for those who wanted fun and relaxation, to a land of fear, anxiety, barbed wire and trenches. One of the first tasks in building a defense was to clear the land and erect barbed wire fences along the beaches, including the famous Waikiki. Bomb shelters and trenches were constructed at schools. Dorinda hated the bomb shelters because they were dark, smelly and full of bugs. The government dictated that private homes build their own bomb shelters. Because every time Dorinda's father dug a hole in their back yard it filled with water, Dorinda's yard did not have a bomb shelter.

Military installations, gun emplacements, and buildings were draped with the brown and green camouflage nets. Some buildings were painted with camouflage. It was common to see sand bags piled in front of buildings with soldiers standing guard with bayonets attached to the rifles. The sharp points on the bayonets terrified Dorinda. She writes in *Pearl Harbor Child*:

"When my school became a military hospital, I went to a school in downtown Honolulu next to the Governor's home. At the entrance to the governor's home were two soldiers with the largest bayonets I had ever seen. These were the two that I feared the most. Every day before and after school, I would cross the street and walk a block out of my way just to avoid looking or even coming close to those guns armed with their long, sharp knife blades."

Because of the fear of a poison gas attack by the Japanese, everyone was issued a gas mask, even to Dorinda and her two year old brother. They were to be carried in a shoulder bag at all times. Dorinda's mask and bag always felt heavy and she did not enjoy carrying it. Dorinda participated in gas mask, and emergency drills. Her favorite drill was to be an injured person lying beside a road waiting for medical care.

Dorinda remembers the blackouts and curfews. No lights could be on after dark, and Dorinda thought is was fun to eat in the dark when she couldn't even see her food. If the patrol saw a light on in a home, they would simply shoot it out. One time Dorinda's mother was almost arrested because she had a flashlight on for only the moments it took for her to put a load of washing in their washing machine on their back porch. Censorship was an important activity carried on at the post office in Honolulu, and no one was to talk about the weather.

Living with shortages

It seemed that there was a shortage of almost everything in Hawaii. According to Dorinda, "Everything was rationed." One of the main shortages was gasoline. Most people were issued gasoline ration stamps that allowed them to purchase five gallons of gas twice a week. If a person's job was critical, such as Dorinda's father, more ration stamps were allowed so they could drive to and from work. Dorinda recalls:

"Eggs were too expensive to buy, and even if you could find meat in the stores, it was too expensive. That was when I first learned to like peanut butter, and beans, both foods that Dad introduced to our family. When we could get peanut butter, Dad would mix the oil off the top into the peanut mixture. At first I thought it was awful, like the beans he used to cook on the back of the kerosene stove. We ate a lot of beans with onions, and even a scrap of ham if we could get some."

Butter was hard to get, but white margarine could be obtained, and colored with a tablet that, when mixed, would turn it yellow. Dorinda remembers spending many nights mixing the white margarine until it turned yellow. Food in tins was hard to find.

Dorinda especially remembers the shortage of toilet paper. "Mom would save paper, usually newspaper," writes Dorinda in her book, "and rub it back and forth against itself to soften it, and that became our toilet paper. There was no way you could call it toilet paper."

Hosiery was hard to find. Many women painted their legs, and drew a seam on the backs of their legs to imitate real stockings, except Dorinda's mother, because her legs were naturally brown. Dorinda, like most of her friends, missed candy and other items which contained sugar. Dorinda missed bubble gum more than anything.

Rubber and metal were in short supply and badly needed to make war equipment. Dorinda went from door to door collecting shoe heels, toys, sink stoppers and bathing caps and turned them in to be recycled for the war effort. She collected tin foil, old pots and pans and other metals to be recycled also.

Most families cultivated vegetable gardens, called "victory gardens". Dorinda's job was to hoe the weeds. She hated it and balked, pouted and complained at every opportunity. When her father started raising rabbits for consumption, Dorinda was very upset. She liked the rabbits and had names for all of them. In order to save the rabbits, "...I began to hoe the garden, and pull the weeds without complaining," recalls Dorinda. Along the way, she learned to like vegetables.

The war years
As the Americans produced more guns, ships and aircraft, it also increased the size of the armed forces. The number of sailors, marines, army, and army air force men (most of whom looked like young boys) soon out numbered the Hawaiian population. These men were either on their way to war, just returning or being treated at hospitals.

These young men swarmed over an area known as "Hotel Street", where they could find many bars, tattoo shops, massage parlors, photo shops and prostitutes. Young Dorinda was forbidden to go into that part of Honolulu. Her parents would not even let her ride a bus through the area.

Dorinda saw her mother, as many children did at the time, spend long hours working for the war effort, and giving hula lessons in the evenings. Dorinda remembers that even at the movies, one could not forget about the war. There were always war newsreels, and even the cartoon characters were in military uniform. Dorinda, along with her mother's hula students, entertained live audiences. Dorinda was amazed at the blue eyelids of the U.S.O. girls. She thought they were beautiful, but for a long time could not figure out how they did it.

Dorinda witnessed many of the Japanese-Americans being interned on Sand Island near Honolulu. She was aware that many were sent to the United States. That episode is another story—a very sad story. Finally, in 1945 the military ended the blackouts and the curfews. During the war years, Dorinda had become accustomed to the sounds and sights of warplanes, of warships, the large amount of military coming and going, and even the stars in the windows of the homes who had loved ones in the service.

On August 14, 1945 those in Hawaii received the news that Japan had consented to surrender. Dorinda's mother felt that she should cancel her evening hula class because her students, many were military wives, would not want to attend. To the contrary, the students wanted to hold class and be together.

After class, Dorinda accompanied her mother in the black ford to drive a student home. In Pearl City they saw crowds of people surrounding the cars, many of them friends and neighbors. People were celebrating the war's end. When a firecracker went off, it frightened Dorinda because she thought their car was going to catch on fire.

People were marching through the streets banging pots and pans together. Firecrackers were everywhere. People were shouting, "The war is over! The war is over!" Air raid alarms wailed without stop. The ships in Pearl Harbor blasted the air with whistles, and brightly colored flares lit the sky over the harbor. People, including strangers, were hugging and kissing each other. The excitement in the air was electrifying. As Dorinda and her mother drove back to their house, they saw a sailor in his white uniform standing in the yard across the street from their house. Dorinda wondered at the time why he was alone, and not celebrating with the crowds. As Dorinda was curiously watching him, he leaned against a tree. His elbow was bent, and his face was in the crook of his arm. Dorinda saw his shoulders and his head quaking, and she knew that he was emotionally overcome, and crying. For him, and young Dorinda, the war was over.

Aftermath

After the war, the US Navy condemned the civilian property on the peninsula. The residents put up a hard fight not to let that happen—but they lost. For awhile, Dorinda's family paid rent to live in the house. Slowly, the people left. Some took their houses with them. During Dorinda's junior year in high school, the family moved to another location where they could still see the harbor, but not as clearly.

Dorinda attended the University of Hawaii. When she was 18 years old she danced the hula on a weekly television show. At about the same time, she won a hula contest which brought her to the mainland for the first time. She ended up marrying and settling in Missouri.

Dorinda Nicholson has also published *Pearl Harbor Warriors* and a DVD *and Remember World War II*. She is available to speak at schools, and civic and professional groups. For more information contact her website: dorinda@pearlharborchild.com

Dorinda and her little brother, Ishmael, wearing gas masks.

Dorinda

Waikiki Beach

Chapter 10

Christl Upchurch
Schweinfurt Germany

Schweinfurt, Germany
In 1939 Schweinfurt, Germany, located on the Main River in the Lower Franconia region of Bavaria, had a population of about 49,300 people. The city, which dates back to at least the year 740, is about 100 miles east of Frankfurt, and 70 miles northeast of Nuernberg. Schweinfurt, in German, means "Pig Bridge" or "Pig Path", because the pigs in the area crossed a small bridge to assemble on a small island where they spent the daylight hours.

On December 29, 1939, the ground around Schweinfurt was still covered with three inches of snow. A glance at a calendar showed that Germany had been at war in Europe for 118 days. In the afternoon of that cold day, Hedi Kiesel, wife of Wilhelm, gave birth to a baby girl whom they named Christl.

Christl's father, Wilhelm, had been called into the German Army. He was university educated and a professional architect. Wilhelm Kiesel never carried a gun while in the army, and like many Germans, never was a member of the Nazi Party. He was fortunate to be home during Christl's birth.

Target Schweinfurt
Since Christl's father was away for months at a time, Christl lived with her mother and her sister Urusla, who was born two years after Christl, in an apartment in Schweinfurt. Christl has fond memories of her mother placing her on the back luggage rack, and

Ursula in a basket on the front of her bicycle, and peddling to visit her grandparents.

Christl's maternal grandmother lived in the small town of Karlstadt about 30 miles from the apartment; and her paternal grandmother in a small village about six miles away named Kuetzberg. Both grandfathers had passed away. In 1941 and 1942 food was rationed and getting harder to obtain in the cities and the family was able to bring fruit, berries and vegetables back from their grandparents' homes.

The citizens of Schweinfurt had always been proud of the industry in their city; especially so, of the three plants that manufactured ball bearings. The war increased the activity of the plants, and Schweinfurt provided 50 to 60 percent of all of the ball bearings used in tanks, aircraft, trucks and other German war machinery. Because of that very fact, Schweinfurt became a priority target for annihilation by the Allied Powers.

The first bombing raid on Schweinfurt occurred during August 1943 when 230 B-17s of the 8th Air Force flew from England. The American fliers were met by over 300 enemy fighters and heavy, accurate anti-aircraft fire. The Americans, at that time, did not have fighter protection because the United States had no fighters with the range that could fly that far and back. Only 184 B-17s out of the 230 dropped bombs on the target, 36 were shot down and there were 341 American casualties.

On October 14, 1943, the 8th Air Force once again bombed Schweinfurt with 291 B-17s. Sixty B-17s were lost along with 639 American casualties. By 1944 the Americans had long range fighters and, therefore, fighter escorts. The USAAF bombed the city during the day, and the British RAF bombed the city at night.

The apartment where Christl lived was equipped with a concrete air-raid shelter. When the siren on the roof wailed, Christl, her mother, and her sister ran downstairs to the shelter. "I hated the loud siren," remembers Christl. "We slept in our clothes night after night because we knew we would have to jump up and run for cover. It just became a nightmare for me."

Schweinfurt is abandoned

During the summer of 1944, Christl's father sent word to his family that living in Schweinfurt was too dangerous. He told them to go live with Christl's maternal grandmother in Karlstadt. The train trip to Karlstadt, which should have taken about an hour and a half, turned into a grueling eight hours. For safety, the train travelled only at night, and it was so crowded with people and the sounds of crying children trying to get out of Schweinfurt, that one had to crawl through the train's windows in order to board, or exit.

In 1944 Germany was experiencing one of the coldest winters in its history; and by this time, Germans were feeling the shortages brought on by war. Coal was very scarce. By government orders, because of the night air raids, boards and blankets covered the windows of the homes, and no lights were allowed. Evenings were spent in total darkness. "By that time," writes Christl, "we did not have much to eat anymore and portions were getting smaller." It was under those conditions that young Christl, absent her father, spent the Christmas of 1944.

One day Christl's mother looked to the sky from the village of Karlstadt and saw the white vapor trails of many bombers. The vapor trails were not beautiful. They were like long, white arrows of death pointing to a target for destruction. She knew they were pointing to Schweinfurt. Since all fire departments in all outlying cities raced to the cities to help, Christl's mother jumped on a fire truck heading toward Schweinfurt.

Christl's mother arrived at their apartment and found it in ruins. Only the front of the building was standing. The remains were still burning. The shelter in the basement where the family used to go was filled with casualties, and many of them were being carried out as she searched for any belongings. Christl's bed was one of only a few pieces of furniture which survived, and it was taken to their temporary housing in Karlstadt.

The next month, February 1945, Christl's father arrived at Karlstadt. He was very ill, thin and weak from malnutrition. He was home for good, and everyone was elated.

More bombing

Near the village of Karlstadt lay the larger town of Wuerzburg. Because Wuerzburg was a major railroad crossing for most all of the trains in Germany, many troops and articles of war moved through the town continuously. Because of that, the town became a military target for the allied bombers. Night after night the sirens wailed and Chritl headed for cover in the basement of her grandparent's house. Christl was too young to understand a lot about the war. "I only knew I wanted the bombing to stop and have more to eat," recalls Christl.

Christl's grandparents' home was very unique. The two story dwelling was built of hand-hued limestone in 1724. The street-level had a dirt floor and was once used as a locksmith shop. It had a dirt basement with its walls lined with canned food, potatoes and homemade salt pickles. In 1945, it also contained blankets, boards to sleep on, and a few pieces of furniture for comfort during the days and nights of hiding from the bombs.

Even though the price to pay for listening to a foreign radio was execution by the German Gestapo, Christl's family hid and listened to the British radio stations, primarily the BBC, because they felt the news on the status of the war was more reliable.

During the late afternoon on April 2, 1945, Christl, her sister, Grandmother and her mother and father had to take cover in the basement because of an air raid. Christl heard very loud explosions nearby. Christl and her sister were crying and holding tight to their mother and father. Then suddenly, remembers Christl, "...followed the loudest boom I ever heard, furniture was falling from the upper floors, stones, and mortar were causing an enormous amount of dust, we could neither breath, nor see and when everything settled, daylight came through a huge opening at the front of the house." Below the front steps, under part of the upper floor, lay part of an exploded bomb, along with Christl's demolished bed. Christl was in tears.

Refuge sought in the woods

Christl's family managed to crawl from the rubble to the outside. Night was settling in, and there was smoke and fire all around them.

Evidently, the aircraft were intending to bomb the rail center in Wuerzburg, but some of their bombs fell on Karlstadt instead.

Christl's family quickly loaded a handcart full of food, clothing and blankets and headed for a pre-designated shelter in the village. When they arrived at the shelter, they found that the shelter was being used as a hospital for wounded soldiers and civilians. There was no room. "I can still hear the screams of the victims being treated by the medics," recalls Christl.

In an effort to spare Christl and her sister further heartache and trauma, her parents decided to walk to a wooded area about five miles away. Although five year old Christl's ears were still ringing from the bomb explosions, the little girl scurried as fast as her little legs would take her past burning houses, trying to complete the five mile walk to the woods before daylight.

About nine days after the bombing episode in the basement of her grandparents' home in Karlstadt, the 42nd Division of the American 7th Army marched into Schweinfurt and took control of the airfield. The adults were now spreading the word that American soldiers were moving toward their area, and they didn't want to be taken prisoners by the "enemy." The word "enemy" struck fear in Christl's heart.

Christl's family was not the only family to flee to the woods for safety. There were other families there, and they shared their food. Christl spent five long days and nights in the cold woods. Finally, several of the refugees decided to go to a small village not far from the woods. When the hungry, tired families arrived in the small town, they were shocked, and afraid. They were met by American soldiers. The soldiers pointed their rifles at them, which were fixed with fearsome looking bayonets.

The refugee families, along with the entire population of the village, were ordered by the American soldiers to gather in front of an old church and raise their hands in surrender. Christl, even though she didn't understand why, kept her hands in the air, too, because her mother told her it might be best if she did. After several hours, the group of civilians was moved to a school building, where they were locked in (but safe) for a couple of days. After their release Christl's family made their way back to Karlstadt and their bomb ruined home.

Military occupation

On May 2, 1945, Germany surrendered to the Allied Powers; and the war was over. Bavaria, the state in which Christl's family lived, became occupied by the American military forces. The American military established a curfew, and began patrolling the streets, randomly searching the German civilians, and the citizens' homes for weapons and fugitives. People were used to seeing American soldiers almost everywhere. "We children were told to stay close to our house and not speak to the "enemy", whatever that meant," recalls Christl.

Upon returning to her grandmother's home in Karlstadt, the family began repairing and rebuilding the bombed house. The upstairs floor, the front façade, and furniture had to be rebuilt. Some of the stones and bricks of the debris were reused. They mixed their own cement, and cut their own boards. When the house was finished, there was a pile of bricks, stones and other rubble that had to be carried away. The family loaded the debris onto a wagon which was pulled by oxen. Christl remembers picking up stones and loading them onto the wagon to be delivered to a dump.

On the way to the dump, a convoy of American tanks loaded with soldiers approached the oxen-drawn wagon from the opposite direction. The excruciating noise of the tanks panicked the oxen and they bolted toward the tanks. As Christl's father tried to control the oxen, their strength threw him against one of the tanks. A tread of the tank grabbed Christl's father and whirled him to the ground.

The American convoy stopped, and soldiers, who thought he was dead, picked up the bleeding and unconscious man and drove him to a field hospital where American doctors administered to him. Christl's father had a severe concussion, double fracture of the skull base, a broken arm and several cracked ribs. When Christl's father returned home from the hospital, his entire chest and left arm were in a cast.

An "enemy's" friendly overture

During the summer of 1945, Christl and her sister, Ursula, were walking to their aunt's hotel-restaurant, from which they sometimes were given left-over food. The hotel-restaurant was now occupied by American soldiers. The girls left their yard and decided to take a peek at the enemy.

As they approached, they saw a soldier standing outside the kitchen smoking a cigarette. The American soldier saw the two girls and waved them over. Disobeying their parents orders, they went to the soldier, and he gave each girl an orange. Neither girl knew what an orange was. The soldier began to peal it. The sisters ran home with their prize as fast as they could.

Once home, both girls were reprimanded. They were also told what an orange was, and where they were grown. After that, Christl, Ursula, their mother, father, grandmother and aunt shared the two oranges.

The next day, Christl and her sister sneaked back to see their new-found friend. This time, he gave the girls chewing gum, something they had never seen before. Even though the soldier and the two girls could not understand the language of the other, the soldier was able to teach the girls how to chew it. The "enemy" and the "conquered" soon became friends.

One day, the girls took the soldier by the hand and led him to their home. Before he left with the girls, he ran into the kitchen and grabbed a full plate of doughnuts. Upon entering the backyard, Christl remembers, "My dad almost fainted when he saw the American soldier led by me, holding the sweets and my sister and I chewing gum."

The soldier, Roemer Swope, from Zanesville, Ohio, was an army cook at the American occupied hotel. Swope became a friend of the family. In return for Christl's mother washing his clothes, he brought the family soap, coffee, cigarettes, candy and all kinds of groceries and leftovers. The family, who found very little food available for their daily meals, was profoundly grateful.

Swope, who left his military bible with the family when he returned to the United States, became a long-time friend. After Christl became proficient in English, she wrote to him until his death in the mid 1980s

A ravaged Schweinfurt

By the end of the war, Schweinfurt was in ruins. Fifty percent of the houses and about eighty percent of the industrial buildings in the city had been destroyed. There were close to 1100 civilian casualties.

When Christl's father returned to Schweinfurt in 1945 to reestablish his architectural business, Christl moved to the city to attend school. She lived with her father's friends until her father could get settled.

At her elementary school most of the textbooks had been destroyed, there was a shortage of teachers, there were no paper or pencils and; they had only slate boards and slate pencils.

Finding enough food to eat was always a problem. For Christl and most of the children, the first meal of the day was cooked at the school by the United States Army. It was the only meal the children had since the very sparse meal of the night before.

None of the children dressed well. Christl's mother knitted her and her sisters skirts, sweaters, dresses and socks. After a garment was even too small after the last hand-me-down, Christl's mother unraveled, stretched and washed the yarn before remaking it into a larger size. When Christl's shoes were too small, her father would cut the toe out so that her feet would have more room. Sometimes, wet socks and other clothing stayed wet all through the school day. Classes were held from 8 to noon, six days a week.

A new Germany arises

By 1948 the food situation in Germany had not improved. Food rationing flourished in the city. Christl and her sister were not getting enough to eat, and their health was suffering. The two sisters, along with many other children, were issued extra food rations from the government to ward off malnutrition.

By mid 1948 the first government since the fall of Germany was formed. The Federal Republic of Germany gave the impoverished German people some hope. The currency was stabilized. Shops, stores, food, and products began to appear. 1949 was a new era. It was the year Christl entered high school (fifth grade).

In 1949 Christl's father had the opportunity to purchase a nice duplex which had one of the sides destroyed by bombs. The house was rebuilt to form one nice home. It was in a nice neighborhood, with cherry, apple and pear trees in the yard. To Christl the new home meant everything. Christl and her sister loved the bathroom, and made it a point to bath every single day. The freedom of not living with non- family members in a two room apartment was exhilarating. She and her sister shared a room with real beds—not the bunk beds that they had shared in their parents' room. Several families in the neighborhood were American military. By 1950 Christl's father was financially able to purchase a car. No longer did he have to peddle a bicycle to work. The sisters were even able to ski during winter vacations in the Alps. It was a wonderful life for Christl. No longer did she have to worry about bombs falling on her, the terribly loud, ear piercing sounds of the sirens, or the scary darkness of a bomb shelter; and no longer did she wonder if she would have enough to eat each day.

The post war years

Christl was taught etiquette at home. She helped her mother cook beginning at eight years old. Good manners at the table were the law in her home. All meals were taken at the dining room table, which was covered with a formal table cloth and napkins. She learned how to drink and behave properly at the table, how to serve wine and the numerous other details associated with gracious dining.

Christl was good academically, too. She studied German, French and English, and graduated from the Wuerzburg International School for Interpreters and Translators. After graduation, she was employed, ironically, in Schweinfurt at a large ball bearing factory.

Aftermath

Christl Kiesel eventually married a highly decorated career American soldier whose last name was Upchurch, and moved to the United States where she became a United States citizen. She has two children and four grandchildren.

In 2006 she published a book titled, *Memories & Recipes*. The book has about 170 pages divided into her life as a child, many authentic German recipes from the "Old Country", and several photographs.

Christl with Mom 1942

Our house after the bomb attack 1944

Schweinfurt in ashes 1945

(One of Christl's favorite German recipes)

CHICKEN SOUP WITH NOODLES AND DUMPLINGS
(Huehnersuppe mit Nudeln and Kloess'chen)

1 large whole chicken	1 stalk of celery
6 to 8 cups of water	1/2 onion
2 Knorr chicken soup cubes	1 small tomato
3 sprigs of Italian parsley	Salt and pepper
1 large carrot (or a handful of baby carrots)	
8 oz. Egg noodles, preferably Amish	

Place the whole chicken, (preferably a free-range), in a large pot of cold water. Add all ingredients except the noodles. Bring to a boil. Immediately turn down heat and simmer for 1 1/2 hours until legs can be pulled away easily. Place chicken on a platter to cool. Remove skin and bones; cut meat in small chunks to be added to the broth. If you don't like that much meat in your soup, use part for chicken salad. Strain the broth, slice the carrot, adjust the seasoning and add the meat and the carrot. In a fresh pot of salted water, cook 1/2 pound of egg noodles, drain and add to the soup.

BUTTER DUMPLINGS

In a small bowl with a wire whip, mix 1/2 stick of soft butter with one whole egg. Make sure the butter and egg are well combined. Then add 1/3 cup of flour, salt and stir until smooth.

Bring your soup to a boil. Using a wet teaspoon, drop small dumplings into the soup and reduce heat to simmer. The dumplings will take about 5 minutes to cook; they are very fluffy and light and they taste heavenly. Serve soup immediately. Sprinkle with chopped parsley, preferably Italian.

Christl with two of her grandchildren.

Chapter 8

Hubert Franz Ferdinand Manthe
Nazi Youth Camp

Manthe was born on February 7, 1932 in the small village of Brenkenhofswalde, Germany, which was located about 300 miles northeast of Berlin. Brenkenhofswalde, which dated back to the era of Fredrick the Great, was a farming community with lush fields surrounded by beautiful dense forests. Manthe was the third child born of four siblings. He had two older sisters and a younger brother. His father was a potato farmer, along with other relatives in the area.

Farming was hard work and included many long days of toil. The family raised animals on the farm, and they smoked their meat. Mrs. Manthe canned what vegetables she could. Young Manthe grew up with animals and remembers that, "the animals became my best friends."

In September, 1939, Germany declared war on Poland, and launched their notorious, deadly *Blitzkrieg* (lightening warfare). Shortly afterward, the local sheriff knocked on the Manthe's door and announced to the senior Manthe that he must report for duty immediately. Poland, east of Brenkenhofswalde, was completely occupied by the soldiers of the German war machine within a few weeks. Manthe's father was part of that campaign.

In the meantime, seven year old Manthe was left to work the farm and bring the potato harvest in. It wasn't easy for a seven year old boy to throw the harnesses on the large Belgium horses, and drive them into the fields to plow the potatoes up. "I grew up very fast," recalls Manthe. Manthe's father was later relieved from military duty because he had to farm his own property, his wife's mother's property, and his father's property.

When Manthe was ten years old, he and another youth from his area were selected to attend a Hitler Youth Camp. His parents had no say in the matter. If they tried, they would be arrested, and there could be dire consequences.

Hitler Youth Camps

Hitler placed a great deal of emphasis on the young people of Germany because they were the future of the country. He expended effort, time and money to ensure that the young people would be loyal to him and the Nazi party. Hitler had established Youth Camps before 1930. But in 1933 he crowded out all other youth groups and gave the priority to his youth groups.

The Hitler Youth groups consisted of five major organizations. The boys ages 6 to 10 belonged to the Pimpfen (The Little Fellows) group, ages 10 to 14 belonged to the Jungvolk (The Young Folk), and ages 14 to 18 belonged to the Hitler-Jugend (Hitler Youth). The girls' organizations consisted of the Jungmädelbund (Young Girls) for those ages 10 to 14, and the Bund Deutsche Mädel (League of German Girls) for aged 14 to 18. Young Manthe belonged to the Jungvolk where he wore a brown shirt and black pants.

The schools were to teach the children to believe in the superiority of the Aryan, or "master race" as they called themselves. They were taught discipline, sacrifice and loyalty to Hitler, their father figure. All books in Germany were banned. In the Youth schools, the textbooks were rewritten to praise the Nazi party. All disasters were blamed on the Communists and the Jews. Children were taught how to spot a Jew by facial characteristics. Jewish teachers and professors were purged from the class rooms, and the rest lived in fear of being labeled a traitor. There was a picture of Hitler on every class room wall.

Throughout the early and mid 1930s the Hitler Youth organizations slowly superseded the traditional elementary and high school systems. Instead of mathematics, science and intellectual curriculum, emphasis was placed on Nazi ideology and physical development. Children recited, verbatim, the ideology which they had been taught. By the mid 1930s the Catholic and Protestant schools had been abolished. Church holidays were not recognized, and prayer was banned from the class rooms. Religion was replaced by Nazi ideology.

By 1940, the British were conducting air-raids over Berlin. The Hitler Youth were called in and put to work as air-raid wardens and assistants to man anti-aircraft guns. As the air-raids worsened, and because of America's entry into the war, some of the Hitler Youth were trained by the German army (Wehrmacht) to operate military weapons. By 1943, about the time Manthe was selected for the Hitler Youth, the shortage of manpower in the cities dictated that anti- aircraft guns (flak guns) would be manned solely by the Hitler Youth.

The young boys manned search lights, and delivered dispatches on their bicycles. In 1943 a search light crew was hit by an Allied bomb which killed the whole crew. The entire crew consisted of boys under 14 years of age. The boys were used for innumerable chores, from cleaning the debris from bombing raids to helping to evacuate Jews.

In an attempt to protect the children of the Hitler Youth, the Nazis set up their schools in the rural areas. These were called Hitler Youth KLV (Kinderlandverschickung) camps. It was one of the KLV camps to which ten year old Manthe was assigned.

Each KLV camp was run by a Nazi approved teacher and a Hitler Youth squad leader. Life inside the camps was of a strict military type discipline. "They were like the basic training courses which the American military endured after their induction to the armed forces," recalled Manthe. The boys learned to obey all orders unconditionally, without questioning. They were taught to snap to attention at any time. They were required to attend roll calls, and to participate in para-military exercises, rugged hikes and marches.
The boys learned to sing Nazi songs.

Sometimes the boys were ordered to march 50 miles without any food other than the concentrated food they carried in the packs. On one occasion a 14 year old boy standing guard duty at a camp shot a 10 year old youth because the youth couldn't remember the password.

Weakness in a boy was despised and ridiculed. Generosity, kindness and sympathy had no place in the rigid philosophy of the training. The rule of the day was, "survival of the fittest." The boys were subjected to being bullied and humiliated. They were abused physically, and sometimes, sexually. However, many boys liked the Hitler Youth because they were fed well, and enjoyed the sports and physical activities.

The boys were taught that their race was superior. They believed that they were the strongest, the bravest and the "best." Many of the feared, dedicated Nazi SS members were recruited from the Hitler-Jugend, which consisted of the Hitler Youth ages 14 to 18 group. One of Hitler's stated goals was that, "The weak must be chiseled away. I want young men and women who can suffer pain. A young German must be as swift as a greyhound, as tough as leather and as hard as Krupp's steel."

A former Hitler Youth recalled, "In the songs we sang, in the poems we recited, everything was bright, shiny and clear, the sun and the earth were ours, and tomorrow so too would be the world."

In Manthe's own words, he says, "I was indoctrinated; I was brain washed." Manthe reached the point where he felt he had to obey no one, including his father, except Nazi authority.

On one occasion, Manthe was to attend a meeting of the Hitler Youth. His father told him that he needed him for some work on the farm. Manthe told his father that he was not going to stay and work. His father reminded young Manthe that he was his father, and that he must do as he was told. Young Manthe relented, and stayed home against his will. When the Hitler Youth found out, Manthe's father came very close to being arrested.

As the war raged on, food for the German army and the civilians became scarce. Government inspectors visited the farms which peppered the country side and counted the animals and the other products which were produced on the farms. They then would calculate how much of their own products the farmers could keep for themselves. For instance; the inspectors would count the cows, and then estimate how much milk they could give a day. Then they would calculate how much of that milk the family needed. The rest was taken by the German government. It was called rationing.

Although the government took much of what was produced by the Manthe farm, Manthe recalls, "We never went to bed hungry."

Manthe becomes a refugee

By 1945 the German war machine was on the run. Fewer German aircraft were seen in the air, and there was a shortage of pilots. The dogged Russian army had pushed its way through Latvia, Estonia and East Prussia. Manthe had watched the refugees from the countries trudge by his village with the few possessions they could carry. Young Manthe even heard the booms and explosions of the big guns in the distinct east; but he never entertained the thought that he would one day be a refugee himself. The Hitler Youth assigned young 13 year old Manthe to lay explosive land mines on the roads and fields which would be traveled by the advancing Russian forces.

Soon, the Russians were firing outside the village of Brenkenhofswalde. The Germans in the area were not safe. Consequently, The Manthe family, along with hundreds of others, decided to flee for fear of their lives.

In March 1945, the Manthe family packed a "covered wagon" with some smoked meat and some canned vegetables. At least half of the load consisted of grain and seed to feed the two horses which pulled their wagon. Manthe remembers, "We waited while my dad went through the farm one more time to check on the animals and other things. When he returned, he was crying." Manthe can still see and hear in his mind that moment over 60 years ago, the tears in his father's eyes, and the bellowing of the cows as they pulled away from their once secure home.

The eleven Manthe family members whose lives centered around the horse drawn wagon were: Mr. and Mrs. Manthe, the grandmother, young 13 year old Manthe's two older sisters ages 18 and 23, and his younger brother who was ten.

The next four weeks was a terrible time in Manthe's life. The winter still lingered in Germany, and it was cold. Many nights he would crawl onto a pile of horse or cow dung in order to feel the warmth so he could sleep. Sometimes they would stop along the road to build a fire; and they would place potatoes in the fire to provide them a hot meal. Most of the roads were narrow "black tops" which snaked along with hundreds of refugees struggling along from day to day.

The "black top" roads were hard on the horses and caused many to go lame. One of the Manthes' horses died from lameness and dehydration, and many times all members of the family were called upon to push the wagon throughout their journey. The refugees stopped at farms along the way to ask for water from cisterns. Sometimes, they would drink from streams or ponds.

Many German soldiers, who were on the run from the pursuing Russian army, joined the long line of exhausted civilian refugees for protection, and to be unseen. The allies were aware of this fact, and the British sent their world famous Spitfire fighters to strafe the helpless line of refugees. According to Manthe, "Many people were killed."

To make matters even worse, young Manthe was suffering depression.

Depression and hunger

Manthe had been indoctrinated with the idea that Germany was winning the war, and that the "superior race" could never be conquered; that Germany would soon rule the world. But as he and his homeless family faced cold, hunger and death with hundreds of refugees, Manthe wondered how such a thing could happen. He began to question his teachings.

His major teacher in the Hitler Youth was a staunch hard-liner Nazi. He epitomized what a true Nazi should be. The boys looked up to him. They respected him highly, and admired the Nazi pin he always wore in his lapel.

One day, during his trek in the long, weary line of refugees, Manthe spotted his teacher. The Nazi lapel pin was nowhere in sight. The teacher was running for his life from the Russians. He blended in perfectly with the other refugees. Manthe, who was already confused, lost all respect for his former Nazi Youth teacher. Germany was losing the war, and Manthe and his family had left their home and all of their property behind. Disrespect and contempt for the German government began to form in the 13 year old's mind. Because of the unfolding of these events, Manthe, at the age of 13, entered into a serious depression; he was disenchanted. His world had been shattered.

As the refugees moved forward, The Germans were blowing up the bridges in order to slow down the advance of the Russian army. As the wave of refugees approached the Oder River, they knew that the bridge was going to be destroyed. "We were able to cross the Oder before it was destroyed," recalled Manthe. "Those who didn't make it had to stay in East Germany." He is still very thankful to this day that his family made it across.

On Easter Sunday 1945, after four weeks of tortuous travel, the Manthes, all with dysentery, arrived in the town of Stübel, Germany. They were directed to a large farm. According to Manthe, "It resembled an old plantation type with a three story house."

The farmer directed the Manthe family to an old cabbage barn. Rats ran rampant throughout the barn, and it was not a good place to live.

The refugee children attended school while sitting on a dirt floor. "To say the least," according to Manthe, "It was quite sobering, and very humiliating, even as a boy of thirteen."

There were so many refugees, and German soldiers, that food was hard to find. The German soldiers, as they did in many countries where refuges assembled, slept in the fields at night in order to stop the hungry from stealing the plants. Refugees, however, did sometimes brave the night and the soldiers in order to steal a few carrots or a cabbage.

The Manthes spent the next few years moving from one farm house to another, sometimes living in horse barns. They lived a harsh life, and there was very little to eat, except what little could be found in the fields.

When Manthe neared the age of 15, he was able to hire out to work for a local farmer. In exchange for room and board, Manthe received grain and potatoes, which he gave to his family for their support.

About a year later, Manthe was able to obtain a job in a coal mine in Bochum, Germany. Manthe worked the coal mine for about two years. Earlier, while working on the farm, Manthe met a German who had been interned as a Prisoner of War in the state of Kentucky, where he had also worked on a tobacco farm. The man spoke highly of America and its people. Manthe was impressed by the man's Chesterfield cigarettes, and his American made canvas, crepe-soled shoes. Manthe decided that he wanted the same things.

Manthe was also impressed by the American soldiers who were stationed in Germany after the war. According to Manthe, "They were kind, considerate, and good ambassadors for America." At age 18, Manthe had set his sights on leaving Germany.

Manthe crosses the Atlantic

When Manthe applied for a visa to the United States at the American Embassy he was told that he would have to wait four years. Being impatient, Manthe applied successfully for a visa at the Canadian Embassy in Hanover, Germany, and shortly afterward boarded an immigrant ship in Hamburg, Germany for Canada. The Canadian government financed his way over, but Manthe had to pay the government back at a later date. Within four or five months, 19 year old Manthe was working in Toronto, Canada on a mushroom farm.

Manthe knew that once he had resided in Canada for a year, he was eligible to transfer his visa to another country. A year later, Manthe had his visa approved to migrate to the United States. Manthe followed a tip he had received and placed an ad in the *Saint Louis Post Dispatch* which read: "Young German needs sponsor." After receiving several responses, he chose two retired, married college professors who had settled in the Ozark country of Missouri to live out their lives as pioneers.

In July 1952, 20 year old Manthe boarded an airplane, with money he had saved, for Buffalo, New York. From Buffalo, he flew to St. Louis, Missouri, where he boarded a train to Jefferson City, Missouri. It was a hot day in July, when Manthe arrived at the train station in Jefferson City. Manthe was hot, hungry and had no money. He was picked up by his foster mother in a 1948 Willis station wagon, and taken to a one room cabin with a dirt floor located near the town of Laurie Missouri.

Manthe looks back on those years as a "wonderful experience" to live with the two Christian-like folks. "They tutored me 24 hours a day," recalled Manthe. "Most of what I know today, I learned from them." Manthe loved living in the woods. He used to sit on the dirt floor with his foster parents and the "hill folk" and spend many evenings singing.

Not everyone in the Ozarks accepted the German immigrant, especially the owner of a skating rink in the area. Manthe was intrigued by the girls in their short shorts and dresses who skated there. Every time he wanted to enter, the owner turned him down. Finally, Manthe asked the man why he wouldn't let him in. The man, who had a crock of moonshine whisky sitting on a step beside him answered, "Cause you're a German." Manthe leaned over, picked up the crock of moonshine, and slugged some down. The owner stared at him for a few moments, and then allowed Manthe to enter. The two of them became very good friends.

In 1954 Manthe was drafted into the United States Army. After basic training, he was transferred to France. While in France, Manthe had two strikes against him when it came to making friends with the French people. Number one, he was a "Yankee", and number two, he was a German. But Manthe prided himself in breaking personal barriers, such as he did with owner of the skating rink in the Ozarks. He organized a bicycle club with about five children. He bought a bike for each of them and they ended up having a wonderful experience. He became friends with the families, "…it became quite a *tear-jerker* when I left to go home," remembers Manthe.

Manthe returns to the Ozarks

After leaving the US Army, Manthe returned to the Ozarks, and enrolled in college at Warrensburg, Missouri with the help of the G.I. Bill. He received his B.A. Degree in Business in 1959. While in college, he met Oraleen, who became his wife, and to whom he is still married. Hubert "Bert" Manthe and Oraleen raised a daughter of whom they are very proud. Manthe's values and work ethics ensured success for the young man. He became a very successful business man, both in sales and as an entrepreneur.

Manthe was the only one in his family to settle in America. Due to the terrible conditions in which his mother and father lived, they both died early deaths. Over 50 years after Manthe left Germany, he returned for a visit. The old potato farm was gone, and the old cemetery could not be found. The complete town, along with its name, had disappeared into the pages of history. But the memories linger. Even today, Manthe, recalling the days of extreme hunger pains, makes certain he has plenty of food in his home.

Manthe is very proud to be an American. He has taken advantage of the freedoms offered to him in America; and in return, he has given to America. Manthe is living proof that the *American Dream* is still alive. The young Hubert Manthe who was a loyal member of the Hitler Youth camps, transitioned into an upstanding American Patriot.

Young Manthe (center) in his Hitler Youth uniform.

BELOW: With his "adoptive parents" in the Ozarks and right, as an older man.

BOOK IV

Underground Evasion

Chapter 11

Francis X. Medina
B-24 Gunner and MIA (Evadee)

The following story is a summary of the book, Ciao, Francisco, written by Frank X. Medina, coauthored by Dorothy B. Marra, and published in 1995. It is now out-of-print. Mr. Medina has graciously consented to allowing me to summarize his story, and to reprint some of the photographs and text from his book.

Background

Francis X. (Frank) Medina was born in Galveston, Texas on May 24, 1924. Medina was the youngest of five children in a Spanish, blue-collar, middle class family. Medina had two brothers and two sisters. He was educated in Catholic elementary and high schools. Medina's mother called him "Javier" using the Spanish word for his middle name, "Xavier".

After high school, Medina enrolled in a Catholic college. The United States had been at war for about a year. Medina was interested in joining the Army Air Force, but his mother was adamant against him flying. Thus, Medina enlisted in the Infantry Reserve. At the end of his freshman year Medina was called to active duty just two weeks before his 19th birthday. The U.S. Army assigned him to the Air Force. He had no choice.

After completing his basic training in Kerns, Utah, Medina was assigned to Aurora, Colorado for aerial armament school. He completed aerial gunnery school in Harlingen, Texas. After graduation, he applied for the Air Force Cadet program. He passed all of his tests and was on the waiting list. But in the spring of 1944, the USAAF washed out all of the men on the cadet program list and assigned them to the infantry, except for those who had special training. Because of Medina's training in aerial gunnery, he was sent to Lincoln, Nebraska to join a B-24 Liberator combat air crew. Medina was labeled an armament gunner, and was assigned to the tail gunner's position. It was also his job, once airborne, to arm the bombs in the bombbay by pulling the safety pins.

From Lincoln, Medina's crew was sent to Boise, Idaho where intensive training welded the crew into an efficient combat unit. From Boise, the crew boarded a train headed toward Topeka, Kansas to pick up a just-off the assembly line B-24. Medina spent much of the train ride on a platform at the rear of one of the cars. He was awed by the majestic beauty of the mountains, the trees and the clear streams. Like many other service men soaking up the quiet serenity of the moment, his thoughts wandered; and he wondered if he would come back from the war.

At Topeka, Medina's crew loaded their new B-24J and took off. Once in the air, the pilot opened the sealed envelope to learn what their final destination in the European theater would be. After stopping in New Hampshire, Newfoundland, the Azores and Morocco, they arrived at their destination in Cerignola, Italy on July 20, 1944. They were assigned to the 15th Air Force, 459th Bomb Group, and the 756th Bomb Squadron.

Aerial combat

For the first seven days they flew crew training missions. After much thought and discussion, the crew formed a consensus of what to name their Liberator. Since five of the crew members were "Yankees" from the North, and five crew members were "rebels" from the South, they named their airplane the *Yankee Rebel*. Painted below the name was the likeness of a barefooted mountain moonshiner.

The *Yankee Rebel* flew her first mission over Budapest. According to Medina, it was a "terrifying foray." The antiaircraft fire was thick and close. During that mission Medina saw a B-24 blow up in a fire ball; and the next moment there was nothing there. The airplane and ten men disappeared. Moments later he saw a

B-24 going down, and counted only six parachutes leave the dying Liberator. The whole scene was nerve-racking. Men, to whom Medina talked and joked with one day, would be gone the next day.

Medina's second mission was over the heavily defended oil fields of Ploesti, Romania. Over the target, shrapnel missed the back of Medina's head by only six inches and cut his oxygen line. He was able to use his emergency tank, which held enough oxygen for only three minutes. After the bombs were dropped, Medina scurried to the center section of the *Yankee Rebel* to use other oxygen tanks, but found that four other positions had lost their oxygen tanks. The group of airmen stood in a group taking turns using the good oxygen tank at the waist gunner's position until the B-24 had descended to 10,000 feet.

The main rudder cables had been severed by flak. Fortunately, the flight engineer was able to splice them to hold long enough until they landed. The *Yankee Rebel* had so many holes in it, that it looked like a sieve. The *Yankee Rebel* was one of the four, out of a squadron of ten B-24s that returned to base that day.

Medina's next 15 missions were over heavily fortified targets. They included Germany, Austria, Northern Italy, Czechoslovakia and Southern France.

Medina's 18th mission was scheduled for August 28, 1944. The morning didn't start out well. When the airmen were told that they were to take a different B-24 on the mission, because *Yankee Rebel* was down for repairs, they were distraught. The *Yankee Rebel* had brought them home safely from 17 missions. To some of the crewmen, it was a bad omen.

It was hot. Medina put on some of his clothing, but not all, yet. If he put all of the garments on they would be soaking wet with sweat before he even got off of the ground. But he would put it on later, because he would need it at 23,000 feet where the temperatures were below zero. He checked out his parachute and looked into his survival gear to see the map of Italy printed on white silk, and the $50.00 in Italian money. The military discovered that making a map out of silk was more efficient than making them out on paper. A silk map could be folded into a much smaller unit, it did not make a noise when folding or unfolding and the ink seemed to be more permanent.

The mission for the day for the crew, minus the bombardier who was sick, was to bomb a railroad bridge in Ora, Italy. It was said to be an easy flight. A "milk run" they called it. It was only about a two and a half hour flight. As the Liberator clawed for altitude, Medina put on his heavy suit, woolen cap, insulated overshoes, glove liners and went into the bombbay to arm the bombs. He then put on his Mae West, covered his rubber vest which was attached to his flak suit, two heavy canvas aprons (which contained heavy steel for protection), earphones, throat mike and flak helmet. He then squirmed into his cramped tail turret. His feet were already feeling the cold temperature.

As they reached the target they received only light antiaircraft fire. They dropped their bombs and headed for home. Medina's nervousness kept him from eating breakfast. Now, he was hungry. As soon as they descended to 10,000 feet, he would remove his oxygen and dive into the Spam sandwiches and hot coffee. The bombers were at 16,000 feet, and about to fly over the city of Rovigo, when the crew heard several bursts. The bursts rocked the B-24. Flak had hit the aircraft between #1 and #2 engines. The bomber dropped out of formation. Suddenly, the bomb bay had a hit. Gasoline was pouring into the airplane from ruptured fuel lines. The fuel ignited and the flames spread faster than the crew could contain them. There was no question about it. The bomber was going down in flames.

The pilot rang the bail-out bell. Medina, overcome with fear at first, was now numb, but followed the emergency procedures which had been ingrained in him through his training. Medina jumped from the fiery coffin and tumbled through the air. When he stopped tumbling, he pulled the "D" ring. The parachute opened, and the result jarred every bone in the 118 pound, five feet, eight inches, 20 year old's body.

Medina is MIA

As Medina floated earthward, he was awed by the beautiful Italian country side below. In the distance he noticed the Adriatic Sea. While still floating downward, he saw a couple of his crew members land, as civilians ran toward them. Medina landed hard among the cornstalks in a large cornfield. He took off his parachute and outer flight gear and buried them the best he could. He was down to his olive drab flight suit.

Medina did not want to be captured. He had a strong desire not to become a prisoner of war. Even though a year before the King's troops stopped fighting with the Fascists, and the Allies controlled Southern Italy; the Po Valley in Northern Italy was controlled by the Nazis and Fascists. The Fascists under Mussolini maintained their ties to Hitler and the Nazis and continued to fight the Allies. There were pockets of resistance by Italian civilians, called partisans, who did all they could to sabotage the Nazis and the Fascists.

Medina ran through the cornfield, putting as much space as he could between himself and where he landed. He moved outside the cornfield to follow a small canal. Suddenly, he saw two girls walking very fast toward him. They excitedly waved him back into the cornfield. When the girls reached Medina, they pushed him even farther back into the cornfield, all the time whispering, "soldati!" (soldiers), "Fascists!" Then the girls scurried away.

As he sat in the cornfield he could hear the machine gun fire as the enemy soldiers fired into the cornstalks trying to kill him. Suddenly, a man in civilian clothes came within eight feet of Medina. The man stopped, and looked around. Medina could see the gun in the man's hand. But, for some reason, the man spoke to other men nearby and walked away.

Medina sat silently in the cornfield for hours. Medina found out later that a man had climbed to the roof of a nearby house, and scanned the cornfield with binoculars. Not being able to see a parachute, he came to the conclusion that no one from the B-24 had landed in the cornfield.

During the evening, the two girls came back to where Medina was hiding and gave him two pieces of hard bread and a small watermelon. Medina discovered in talking with the girls that several Spanish words were similar to the same words in Italian, and that he was able to communicate a little. The girls took his high school ring. But when they asked for his watch, he refused. They told him that their names were Erminia and Severina Rosso, and that they lived in the house near the cornfield. When he told the girls that he was going to start walking, they were insistent that he not do so. The girls told Medina "Ciao," (pronounced Chow) and left.

When it was dark, Medina left the cornfield, and with the aid of his map started walking toward Trieste, Yugoslavia. He walked for a couple of hours, crossed through a couple of canals and finally found a cornfield to hide in for the night near the village of Beverare. He was awakened at day break by the talking and singing of the farm workers.

Medina lay there all day, afraid to stand up and be seen. He did scoop up some stagnate water and use the disinfectant pills in his emergency kit to make some drinking water. He thought of home. He prayed. He even sobbed.

Late that night Medina left the cornfield and walked through the darkened streets of the village. Suddenly, two young men in military uniform jumped from the shadows. Medina thought he was caught. The men made gestures of shooting an airplane down, and floating parachutes. They asked him if he was an American flyer. When Medina nodded his head in a "yes" fashion, and mimicked eating, they motioned for him to follow them.

He was taken into an Italian home where the lady of the house fed him salami, hard bread, milk and water. The two young men had been in the Italian army, and after the King surrendered, they kept their uniforms. Soon, a man who was only a year older than Medina entered the house. He told Medina that his name was Ottorino Masiero. Medina, in Spanish, told Ottorino that his name was Francisco (Frank) Medina. After thanking the lady in Spanish, Medina was led out into the darkness by Ottorino.

Ottornio led Medina to a sweet potato field where he revealed a cleverly dug cave beneath the sweet potato vines that Ottorino and his brother had built to hide from the Germans who were conscripting workers for labor camps. The hole was about eight feet long, six feet wide and four feet deep. Boards and potato vines would be used to cover the hole. That night Ottorino brought him Italian clothes. Medina kept his boots and dog tags. Ottornia told Medina that he was lucky to be able to speak Spanish, and could communicate. Ottornio told Medina that he looked like an Italian. Soon, Medina met Ottorino's brother, Vito.

Medina was brought one good meal a day. His Italian was improving. The Masiero family insisted that he not leave the potato patch. They told him that many Nazis and Fascists were in the area, and that the people living next to them, including his uncle, in the duplex farm home were Fascists. Medina could hear the rumbling of tanks of the German army as they passed through the town. On September 10th, 13 days after bailing out of his Liberator, Medina thought of his mother because it was her birthday. Little did he know that only two days earlier she had received a telegram from Western Union.

It read: THE SECRETARY OF WAR EXPRESSES HIS DEEPEST REGRET THAT YOUR SON CORPORAL FRANCIS X. MEDINA HAS BEEN REPORTED MISSING IN ACTION SINCE 28 AUGUST OVER NORTHERN ITALY. Mrs. Medina was near hysteria. She sobbed uncontrollably.

As winter arrived, the potato patch hideaway became cold, and sometimes water-soaked. The Masiero family felt they had no choice but to move Medina in with them, even though the Fascist uncle lived next door. Medina moved in and was put in a hole covered by a cabinet in the kitchen of the house. He met Ottorino's mother and his two young sisters. The complete family was at high risk. They would all be shot if caught harboring Medina. The family, especially the mother, treated Medina like a member of the family.

The partisans in the area were becoming troublesome to the Nazis and the Fascists. More than once they came by the house looking for partisans. On one occasion they searched the Masiero's house room by room. All the while Medina was hiding under the kitchen floor. The presence of the German army was nearer and greater, and there was talk of the Germans taking over peoples' home to house their men; and Ottorino believed that his Fascist uncle next door was suspicious. Ottorino concluded that Medina had to be moved.

In the middle of November, Medina was moved to a barn on the property of the Russo family who owned the cornfield where Medina had landed when he bailed out. He and a man named Matteo, the same age as Medina, shared the hideout. The man had once been brutally tortured by the Fascists, and he had the loss of fingernails to prove it. In order to deceive the enemy, every night they would move from barn to barn. By the end of November, they were grateful for the warmth of the body heat from the horses and other animals with which they shared the barn.

Finally, Matteo, who was later killed, introduced Medina to the 24 year old head of the partisan group in the area named Oreste Zangirolami. Oreste took Medina, who was called "Francisco," to his home and introduced him to his mother, Nina, his father, Primo, his 20 year old sister, Severina, his 22 year old sister, Antinesca, and his 16 year old brother, Terzo. They built an escape route by making a small hole in the wall behind his bed that led into an animal shed. Medina stayed inside the house and kept away from the windows.

By January 1945 Medina had joined Oreste's partisan group. Most every night they went out to look for guns and ammunition, and to recruit partisans. Later they robbed Fascists of money to help the partisan cause. On the nights that Medina and Oreste were not involved in partisan activities, they collected fire wood. At one point Oreste's house was searched. Medina was hidden under the body of one of the Zangirolami's daughters as she lay in bed covered up with blankets.

Because the enemy was pursuing the partisans more every day, and even finding some and killing them; a plan was formed to lead Medina out of Italy. False identification papers were forged, including an official profile portrait. The plan was never implemented.

Medina became like another family member in the Zangirolami household. Mrs. Zangirolami treated him like her own son. He was looked upon as a brother by the siblings. During the eight months of evading the enemy, Medina had learned to communicate in the language; and he learned to love Italian food. He enjoyed drinking wine and singing with the family. If there ever was a family where the men, women and children were touched by war, this was a perfect example.

Rescued

The Allied armies were pushing into the area. The enemy marched daily by the house. Nazis, Fascists and partisans were becoming nervous and trigger-happy. Some of the soldiers were shot by the partisans when they found them isolated from larger groups.

On April 26, 1945 the word spread that the Allies were on the road and would be passing on the road behind the Zangirolami house. It wasn't long before Medina saw the British 8th Army passing by. "Francisco, you are saved," shouted Severina. Mrs. Zangirolami said, "Run, Francisco, catch them. Francisco and Oreste ran after the British convoy. Francisco was running along side a military personnel carrier yelling and waving his dog tags. The vehicle pulled off on the side of the road and stopped. The soldier in charge asked Medina what it was he wanted. Medina told him that he was an American flyer who had been shot down in 1944. The soldiers looked at Medina. He certainly looked like an Italian. But his dog tags and Texas drawl was strong proof that he was who he said he was. The soldier told Medina to get in and that they would take him to their headquarters to verify his story.

Once on the personnel carrier, Medina looked back at the house that had become his home. He saw the Zangirolami family. They were all waving, and shouting, "Ciao (Goodbye), Francisco!" Medina' eyes were filled with tears.

Oreste planned to meet Medina at the British headquarters. After all, the proper goodbys were never said. There were no last-time hugs. But circumstances never let that happen. Medina and his Italian family were deeply disappointed about that fact for years.

Medina's identity was verified, and he was flown to Ravenna in a Piper Cub. From Ravenna he was flown in a B-24 to the 15th Air Force's Headquarters in Bari, Italy.

All this time he was still dressed as the Italian, Francisco. Many times he was asked by soldiers who he was, and he tried to explain.

At Bari he was deloused and issued a new uniform. Medina was again Corporal Frank X. Medina. Francisco was gone, forever. His request to have money delivered to the Masieros and Zangirolamis families was honored by the American government. Medina was promoted to a staff sergeant. The Medina family back in Texas was jubilant when they received a letter from him telling them that he was alive and well. Medina was discharged from the USAAF on October 23, 1945.

Medina completed his college and accepted a job in Dallas, Texas as an industrial engineer. After a while, he accepted a new job and moved to Kansas City, Missouri. It was in Kansas City that he met, and later married Jackie Bartlett. Together they sired four girls and four boys.

After retirement Medina decided to write his story, and he needed to go back to Italy to verify some facts. After all, he had never celebrated his survival with the Zangirolamis.

Italy revisited

In May 1994 (fifty years after he had left Italy), Medina and his wife, Jackie, returned to Italy. Oreste and Terzo met them in Milan. Because of death threats from many people in the Ca Tron community who resented the Zangirolamis partisan activities during the war, the Zangirolamis moved away. Oreste was a successful business man who owned his own furniture and appliance business. Oreste had married Erminia Russo, one of the first little girls to help him in the cornfield. Terzo had done well and was retired. Terzo still had the silk map which Medina had given him. Medina was able to visit the two girls, Antinesca and Severnia, both in their seventies. Mr. and Mrs. Zangirolami were now deceased.

Medina and his wife met members of the Masiero family, and the homes in which he had hidden during the war. Much had changed. While gazing at the old homes, the canal and the cornfield (which was still a cornfield), memories clouded his mind. He was thankful to be alive.

As Medina's modern jet airliner climbed for altitude on its way to New York, Medina looked down on the Italian landscape with fondness. He thought of the Italian people he loved, and he knew that they loved him, too. His thoughts returned to a story that the Zangirolami sisters had told him a few days before his departure. According to the sisters Mrs. Zangirolami was on her deathbed in 1978. Her four children, Oreste, Terzo, Severina and Antinesca were at her bedside. Mrs. Zangirolami softly murmured that one child was missing. Her children answered her that all of them were there. When Severina asked her mother who was missing, her mother softly answered, "Francisco."

The following poem was presented to Medina when he graduated from aerial gunnery school by his sister Josie. Medina has never been able to identify the author.

"The Gunner"

You can talk about the crew chief
Or the doughty bombardier
Or the radio operator
With the educated ear.

You can laud the skilled mechanic
And the navigator, too.
Or brag about the pilot
Till your face is set and blue.

You can tell about their exploits
Over Rome or Dover Straits,
The Solomons, New Guinea
Or wher'er they dared the Fates.

You can sing the praise of every man
Who ever wore a 'chute.
And all those in the air crew,
And the hanger crew to boot.

But when the going's really tough
And a Zero's on your tail
Or a Heinkel's high above you
And the lead comes down like hail

Who's the guy you look to
When your life's not worth a dime?
It's the clear-eyed, tightlipped gunner
It's the gunner every time.

Sure it's fine to be a pilot,
And wear those wings upon your chest
But it's fine to be a gunner, too,
When o'er some cloudy crest

Comes a flight of hell-bent Nazis
With plain murder in their eyes
And a burning half-crazed purpose
That's to knock you from the skies.

That's when your pulse thumps madly
And you wonder what's ahead.
Will you end your mission safely
Or be named among the dead?

Will your bomber wing back homeward,
Every crewman at his post?
Or be shot down, shattered, flaming,
To inspire a Nazi boast?

You can think a thousand things like that,
When the slugs begin to wail
Unless there's one your faith is in;
The one you know won't fail.

He's the guy you look to
When your life's not worth a dime;
He's the clear-eyed, tightlipped gunner
Yes, the gunner every time.

MIA INFORMATION

All men who did not return from combat duty were initially listed as MIA--Missing in Action. As additional information was received, the category was changed to one of the following: KIA, meaning Killed in Action; POW, meaning Prisoner of War; Escapee, meaning one who escapes from captivity and returns to his base; and Evadee, meaning one who evades the enemy and returns to his base, as did Corporal Medina.

A survey of Missing Air Crew Reports (MACRs) from the 459th Bomb Group in which Medina served, indicates that for a 14-month period near the end of World War II - from March 2, 1944 through April 26, 1945 - 993 men were lost in combat. Of these, 445 became POWs; 279 were KIAs; 81 returned from friendly territory; 39 were internees in neutral territory and 149 evaded the enemy. Corporal Medina was one of these 149, as he went down on August 28, 1944. (This information courtesy of Mr. Lyle McCarty, Historian for the 459th Bomb Group Association.)

From a list of approximately 100,000 men reported Missing in Action over Europe in World War II, most were either Killed in Action or Prisoners of War. Medina was one of only a few thousand who evaded the enemy and eventually returned to their units. (This information courtesy of Mr. Clayton C. David, Membership Chairman of the Air Force Escape and Evasion Society. AFEES was formed in 1964, and in 1994 had over 900 members. The Society is in contact with 700 benefactors who aided MIAs in their evasion of the enemy.)

Severina Zangirolami

Antinesca Zangirolami

The Zangirolami home, now vacant, near Ca Tron in the Po Valley, where I lived as an MIA during the winter and spring of 1944-1945. (Photo May 1994)

Oreste Zangirolami, left, and his brother, Terzo, display the silk map of Italy that I gave to them when I left in April 1945. (Photo May 1994)

Medina's photo on his false identity papers.

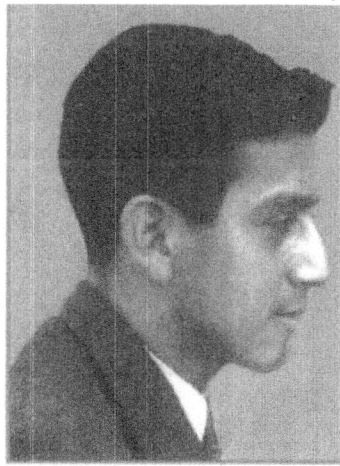

Medina home from the war.

Chapter 12

Nikolas "Nick" Willems
Underground in the Netherlands

Nick Willems was born in the south part of the Netherlands near the Belgian border in 1924. He was one of eight siblings. He had four brothers and three sisters. When Nick was about six years old, his father, a high school teacher, moved his family to a city named Schiedam, a town a few miles from Rotterdam in central Holland in order to provide broader educational opportunities for his children.

In Schiedam, Nick's father taught history and art. His mother remained home to take care of the family of ten. The senior Willems provided for a maid to help with chores. Nick entered high school at the age of eleven, and rode his bicycle 10 miles each way to and from school. In fact, everyone in the family rode bicycles. The family had a shed where the bicycles were lined up when they were parked. Nick remembers his young years with his family as busy and happy.

During the middle 1930s, Nick's family listened to the ranting propaganda speeches of Adolf Hitler as he began his ambitious plans of expansion through Europe. The Netherlands was still trying to regain its economic strength from the disastrous world wide depression of the 1930s. Poverty and unemployment were common, and the military budget was cut in order to conserve money.

It wasn't until the Germans remilitarized the Rhineland in 1936, that the Netherlands finally increased their military budget.

The Williams' family continued to listen to the radio reports as Germany annexed Austria and occupied the Sudetenland in 1938. Nick remembers the elation of Neville Chamberlin when he espoused the notable line, "There will be peace in our time."

When the German war machine pushed into Poland on September 1, 1939 with its devastating *Blitzkrieg* (lightening war), and Poland folded after three days, the Netherlands had still not mobilized their army or navy. In fact, they did as they had done in WWI; the Netherlands declared its neutrality. Once Great Britain and France declared war on Germany, the Netherlands mobilized their meager forces.

Germany invades the Netherlands

Finally, on May 10, 1940, while many of the Dutch people who never believed the Germans would invade the Netherlands, watched as the Germans marched, drove and dropped from the skies in parachutes to occupy their country. Sixteen year old Nick Willems, who was involved in his high school finals, watched as the "German paratroopers fell from the sky" over Rotterdam. Germany had expected to take the Netherlands in a day, and was surprised by the resistance which the small Dutch army, armed with WWI weapons, showed.

The German *Luftwaffe* (air force) bombed Rotterdam, and by May 15, 1940, the Dutch army surrendered. The invasion resulted in 3,500 dead, 6,000 wounded Dutch soldiers, and more than 900 Dutch civilians killed. The German army had 2,500 soldiers killed, 6,000 wounded and 700 reported as missing.

In Schiedam, Nick was living a fairly normal life for awhile. His father, however, became very ill. Because of the possible lack of income due to the illness of his father, Nick could not afford to attend the University. Instead, he enrolled in a technology institute to study engineering. Because the Nazi government released the Dutch soldiers, if they promised not to engage in activities against the Germans, the technology institute was filled with former Dutch soldiers and officers.

The former military men intrigued Nick. "For the first time in my life, I discovered the difference between military and civilians," recalls Nick. "They were different from civilians. They were tough. If they didn't like a teacher, they gave him a hard time. Many of them eventually went into the Dutch resistance."

According to Nick, "The first year, the Germans were very nice, very friendly. If a lady got on the street car, a German soldier would stand up and offer her his seat." But most women would not accept it because they felt the soldiers were insincere. Only a small number of the Dutch were National Socialists (2%), and only a few were Nazi collaborists.

By 1943 the Nazi occupiers began to tighten the collar around the Dutch. A teacher who would not toe the line was fired. Jews were still wearing the Star of David which they had been ordered to wear in 1942, the young Jewish children could not go to school, and Jewish businessmen had their shops shut down. By 1943 Jews were being sent to internment or concentration camps. Of the 140,000 Jews who had resided in the Netherlands prior to the invasion of 1940, only 30,000 survived the war.

The persecution of the Dutch Jews by the Nazis, along with the *arbeitseinsatz* (forced civilian work parties) began to have a profound effect upon the evolution of Nick's mind. It started by forcing every person 16 years of age to attend a semi-military training camp. Many refused. Every man between the ages of 18 and 45 was required to work in German factories, if called. Many of these factories were being heavily bombed by the Allies.

Because food was sent out of the country to support the Nazis, rationing was implemented in the Netherlands. Ration cards were taken away from those who violated German laws. All of these factors weighed heavily on the young patriot's mind, and Nick made the decision to go "underground."

Nick goes "underground"

There are two terms, *resistance* and *underground,* which some people do not understand. Resistance groups consist of people who are armed and engage in fighting, killing, sabotage or any activity against their occupiers in order to harass, or defeat them. According to Nick, "Underground people were people who disappeared, or hid." Many times, the two overlapped.

By 1943 Nick had enrolled in the University. When he enrolled for the second semester of his sophomore year, there were some requirements that bothered him. For one thing, he had to sign a paper stating that he was not a Jew. Another was the requirement that during the summer vacation of the university, students would spend that time working for the German war industry. Eighty percent of the students refused to sign, and were kicked out. Universities were shutting down partly or completely all over the Netherlands. Another law stated that any student who had not signed the declaration must report to the police station and sign one, or they would be kicked-out of the university and be forced to go and work in Germany.

Nick lay in bed at night thinking about all of the things confronting him. "I was scared," recalls Nick. Consequently, in 1943, 19 year old Nick Willems made the decision to go underground. He told a sister that he was going to leave. She was the only one who knew where he was going. He did not want to tell his parents, because if they were picked up by the police, he wanted them to truly not know where he was.

The resistance helped locate people who would risk their lives to engage in "people-hiding." Refugees, Jews, (Ann Frank), underground operatives, draft age Dutch and Allied fliers were harbored. When Nick left his home in Schieham he traveled to a potato farm about one hundred miles east, north of the town of Arnhem, where, in 1944, the well known battle took place and was publicized by the movie, "*A Bridge Too Far*." The farmer who hid Nick had seven children of his own. Even though the farmer knew that the penalty for hiding people was deportation or death, he harbored Nick, anyway. Later, Nick's brother, who was studying to be a minister, showed up on the same farm.

One day Nick was not in the fields. He was lying on his bed because he did not feel well. Suddenly, German soldiers, referred to as Jewish commandos because they hunted down Jews, entered the farm. Someone informed Nick that the Germans were coming in. Nick bolted out the back door and ran for the safety of the fields. The Germans started shooting at him. He was grabbed by a couple of the soldiers who beat him with a revolver. Nick's brother, who was working in the garden, was also captured.

Nick produced his registration papers upon request. His papers, of course, had been forged by the underground. "The

Germans knew my brother and I were city boys who had gone underground," says Nick. "But the Germans had orders to find and arrest Jews, and were not authorized to arrest us. But that's typical of how the Germans operated. They strictly followed orders." So the Germans called the police to have a unit pick up Nick and his brother the next day. Of course, when the next day arrived, Nick and his brother were gone.

Nick fled to another village where underground refugees including several Jews and resistance fighters were hidden. Again he stayed on a farm. The partisans at city hall had changed his papers and his name. His new name was now Jan de Ruyter, who was a famous Dutch general. Nick's first name was given to a Jewish man. Every time someone would call for Nick, now the Jewish man, Nick would, instinctively, want to answer.

By 1943 and 44 the Germans cracked down hard on the Dutch. When some of the Dutch farmers refused to deliver milk or produce to the Germans as ordered, the Germans would go to the farm and shoot the farmer.

Another method the Germans used in order to force discipline on the Dutch, was to take the village or town notables, such as mayors and other leaders, and place them in a hostage internment camp. Then, if a person in the resistance killed a German, the Germans would kill one or more of the Dutch notables in the internment camps. Nick's uncle, who was a mayor of a town, was held in one of the Germans' internment camps for two years, but, fortunately, was never chosen to die because a German was killed.

Sometimes the Germans would kill many for the death of a few, or even, one. In 1943 when some Dutch resistance activists rang the doorbell of a Dutch collaborator named Hendrik Seyffardt, they shot him to death when he answered the door; SS General Hanns Rauter killed 50 Dutch hostages and raided the universities. In 1944 when Dutch resistance fighters attacked the SS General's car, over 250 Dutch hostages were murdered. In another incident, when the Dutch resistance attacked a group of soldiers near the village of Putten, the entire male population of Putten was killed or taken to a concentration camp where most of them died. By these actions, the Germans were earning the undying hatred of the Dutch people.

Nick was gaining experience in hiding and his intuition was sharpening. He did not feel safe in the second village, and he thought he would be better off if he left, which he did. It wasn't long after Nick's departure that the Germans descended upon the Village in which Nick had stayed. The Germans, who had been looking for underground people and Jews, surrounded the village, and rounded up all of the young men and boys. They placed the young men in a church, and ordered them all to undress completely.

No matter how much a young man would lie about not being Jewish, once he undressed, his circumcised penis would always give him away. Knowing this, the same Jewish boy in the group which had Nick's name, managed to escape from the church. After the war, when Nick returned to the farm for a visit, the farmers were still talking about the naked Jewish boy running through the country side from one farm to another seeking a farmer who would hide him.

Nick's next hiding place was in the house of a pastor. Even then recalls Nick, "The Germans were still hunting for people." One day as Nick was riding a bicycle through the country side, he came upon a police officer. As the two approached each other, Nick looked at the police officer, hoping that the officer would not stop him. But the officer did stop him, asking for his papers. Nick was nervous. He decided that if the officer wanted to question his forged papers, or arrest him, "…that I would knock him out." The officer looked at Nick's papers, handed them back, and told him to have a good day.

Eventually, Nick left the pastor's house. At one time he slept in the woods, alone, for about two months. It was cold and damp and he slept on the ground. A nearby farmer brought food to him once a day. In the meantime, more Germans were coming into the country to help build a stronger defense against the expected invasion by the Allies. By 1944 the Dutch people were starving, and feeling more unsafe than ever. Because the city of Schiedam was becoming unsafe, Nick's mother, father and his remaining siblings left their bomb damaged home and were evacuated to The Hague. Later they moved to a farm, where they at least could find enough to eat. It was the same farm where Nick and his brother had stayed when he first had gone underground. By 1944, Nick thought that the farms had become more crowded and very unsafe.

The Germans needed all of the manpower that they could muster for the expected Allied invasion, and they were hungry, too. Thus, he decided to go back to The Hague to live with one of his sisters, two men who were brothers who were also in the underground and the maid. The maid trekked from the house to the authorities to secure coupons that would allow them to go to a "soup kitchen" which the Germans had established. The coupons allowed each person a bowl of soup and a piece of bread. "Because my parents had hoarded some food and had sent us their coupons," says Nick, "we were able to survive."

Prior to the time his parents moved to the farm, an older brother, who lived in the east, invited Nick to join him to study the architecture of old buildings in The Hague. According to Nick, "My brother had good papers and I felt somewhat safe." One day as Nick and his brother were in The Hague, two German Gestapo soldiers walking behind them stuck a gun in their backs and told them to go with them. Nick and his brother were taken to the Gestapo headquarters.

As the two brothers walked into the Gestapo headquarters, an electronic door closed behind them. Nick was worried, because his papers stated that he was Jan de Ruyter. Fortunately, the brothers had prepared themselves for such an occasion, and knew that they could not reveal that they were brothers. According to Nick, "fortunately, we didn't look alike." They told the Gestapo that they were looking at historical buildings.

The Gestapo inspected Nick's brother's papers. They looked good. The Gestapo called the hometown listed on the papers. Everything checked out. When the Germans placed a call to the city listed on Nick's papers, they couldn't get through because it was Sunday; so they released both of them.

While living with his sister in The Hague, Nick was seeing a girl friend, which he had known from high school. The girl's parents had a large enough house, that the Germans had requisitioned the downstairs to house some army officers. Nick used to walk to the girl's house which was in a small town southwest of The Hague. Sometimes he would stay overnight upstairs, and, according to Nick, "I could hear all of those Germans downstairs partying and drunk; a strange bunch." Later, Nick's girlfriend's father was transferred by his job to Arnhem, in the province of Gelderland.

Germany crumbles

Nick remembers seeing and hearing the British Lancasters flying over, night after night, to bomb the harbors which were under Nazi control. Although it was against the law to listen to the radio, the Dutch managed to huddle around their secret radios and listen to the British Broadcast Company (BBC) report on the war. The great assault in June by the Allied Forces at Normandy led the way for the allies to advance toward the Netherlands. It was obvious to the Dutch people that Germany was in trouble; and the Dutch were ecstatic.

During September 1944 the Allies launched Operation "Market Garden" in order to advance into northern Netherlands and Germany. The attempts failed at the time because the British forces could not take the bridge at Arnhem; and therefore were not able to cross the Rhine River and move on to northern Netherlands and Germany. The landing of the British paratroopers at Arnhem was a disaster, with about 16,000 British causalities. Many were just slaughtered because of the unexpected presence of two Pfanzer (armored) divisions. The battle was portrayed in the movie, "*A Bridge Too Far*". When Nick revisited Arnhem in late 1945, he observed that they were still in the process of digging up the bodies of dead soldiers. In April of 1945 the Allied forces crossed the Rhine at Arnhem.

Much of the southern part of the Netherlands had been liberated by September of 1944. Eventually, because the Dutch people in the west were starving, the first condition for possible surrender talk was dropping food in western Holland. Allied aircraft flew over and dropped food on certain designated fields. Nick remembers the food falling from the sky. It was mostly dried food, and included such things as biscuits, dried beef and powered milk. According to Nick, "Some of the starving people ate so much that they killed themselves."

The German forces in the Netherlands finally surrendered on May 5, 1945, just three days before Germany surrendered to the allied forces on May 8 (VE-Day).

Freedom regained

The Netherlands suffered the highest death rate per capita, of any of the other western European countries occupied by the Nazi regime. The count at the end of war tallied a total of 205,900 Dutch men and women, not counting another 30,000 who died at the hands of the Japanese in the Dutch East Indies.

The Nazi invasion and occupation of the Netherlands left many bitter feelings in the hearts of most of the Dutch people, and they had no sympathy for their countrymen who had collaborated with the Nazis. Men who had served with German military units were used to clear some of the many mine-fields laid by the Germans. Some of these men were killed performing the tasks. Dutch women, who had sexual relations with the Germans, were punished and humiliated in public by the Dutch. Nick remembers seeing women who were positioned in chairs being hauled through the streets on trucks, with their heads shaved and red swastikas painted on their heads.

There are two memories which are indelibly sketched upon Nick's mind more than any others. One occurred when he was 16 years old living in Schiedam. "It was such a strange feeling," remembers Nick, "when I first saw two German soldiers walking through my home town. It was just a shock-feeling to see someone from a strange nation in a uniform you don't know."

The other incident occurred in Rotterdam just two days before the complete surrender. The Germans were told to lay down their arms. A group of Dutch resistance fighters approached a group of German soldiers, some of which were SS troops, and told them to lay down their arms. Instead of laying down their arms, the Germans shot all of the resistance fighters in cold blood.

Nick recalls a time when the Dutch were waiting for their liberators, when a column of German soldiers, who had laid down their arms, were walking to a designated location to surrender. The Dutch people did not say a word. As the German soldiers passed, the Dutch silently turned around with their backs to the German column.

When the first victorious Canadian soldiers did finally move through the towns, the Dutch were elated. Nick's girlfriend, Ineke, (his future wife) jumped on a Canadian tank and rode to another town. After she had hitchhiked back, she brought cigarettes to appease her father. "After the liberation," recalls Nick, "we partied, and partied and partied some nights; we never went to bed."

After the liberation, Nick pedaled his bicycle 100 miles to the farm where his parents were. None of the Willems family knew who was still alive. He met his parents and they left the farm.

Aftermath

Nick finished his degree in civil engineering at the university in 1946. Two years later he married; and he and his wife, Ineke, moved to Pretoria, South Africa where they worked for the government, and later for a consulting engineering firm. They lived in Africa for 12 years and had four children. It was obvious to Nick and his wife that a great many serious political and social problems were forming on the horizon in Africa; and in 1960 Nick and his family moved to the United States. Nick did not have a desire to move back to the Netherlands because of what he referred to as a rigid, layered type of social structure. He earned a PhD at the University of Kansas in engineering and taught civil engineering at Kansas University for 30 years before retiring. In the meantime, Nick and his wife adopted a young teenager.

They became very active in the Mustard Seed Church and Nick spent 20 years as the Senior Pastor. One of his sons, who lives next door, is now the Senior Pastor. Even after Nick stepped down as Senior Pastor, he remained active within the church teaching, working with the alpha out-reach program; and publishing Bible stories. His wife of 54 years, whom he so adored, is now deceased, and he shares his home with a foreign student.

He became an American citizen, and firmly believes that America is truly the land of opportunity. In a return visit to the Netherlands in 1954, he visited his home town and the farm to which he first fled in the underground. While there, he heard some man speaking German, and the memories of feelings of fear and resentment of the Nazi occupation overwhelmed him. Those memories still exist in Nick's mind.

Rotterdam after bombings by Germany in 1940

Nick Willems (third from right, in back)

Nick Willems in 2008 at 84 years old

BOOK V
Proud to Serve

Chapter 13

William "Bill" Davis
P-51 Pilot

Heart of America Wing member William "Bill" Davis grew up in Topeka, Kansas and graduated from Topeka High School. Shortly after graduation, his father passed away and because of a shortage of money, Davis entered the work force instead of enrolling in college. Davis's father's former boss, a WWI pilot, prompted Davis to enlist in the USAAF, and was able to secure five top recommendations for Davis to enter the pilot training program without any prior college.

After taking the required tests in Kansas City, and passing by one point, Davis traveled to Santa Anna, California where he was classified for pilot training. He took his primary training in Blythe, California flying PT-22s, then to Arizona for basic, flying BT-13s and on to Luke Field near Phoenix for advanced flying in AT-6s.

From Luke Field, Davis was sent to March Field to check out in the Lockheed P-38 Lightning. At March Field Davis was given a cockpit check in the Lightning, and then told to take off and get the feel of it. An instructor told Davis to remember to push both throttles together at the same time. "I took off," recalls Davis, "and it wasn't too bad. I went up and fooled around for awhile until they called me to return to the base immediately because of a severe cross-wind coming in. By the time I reached the landing pattern the cross-wind was there." Davis brought it in successfully and felt pretty good about landing a strange airplane in a strong cross-wind.

Shortly afterward, Davis was told to report to Portland, Oregon to join Colonel Martin's 354th Fighter Group flying Bell P-39

Airacobras. Davis enjoyed flying the P-39, even though he almost lost his life in a tumble-spin.

The life-numbing experience began when Davis was practicing maneuvers with other P-39s. The P-39's engine was located behind the pilot's cockpit. This configuration sometimes, under certain conditions, caused the airplane to go into what was called a tumble-spin. About a dozen pilots on the west coast had already been killed because they got into a tumble-spin and couldn't recover. According to Davis, "They had no idea of how to get out of the tumble-spin. They told us to do the normal spin recovery procedures, and pray."

During this particular flight, the leader executed a loop. Davis was the fourth behind the leader to execute the loop. As Davis neared the top of the loop, he could tell that he wasn't going to make it. "I should have rolled out," recalls Davis, "but I thought, well, maybe I could make it." The next thing Davis felt was a violet shaking of the airplane. He was in a tumble-spin. He went through the recovery: pulled back the power, hit the opposite rudder, and popped the stick straight forward. Nothing happened. He did another recovery. Nothing happened. "The plane was shaking me all over the place," remembers Davis, "and the stick was going back and forth just beating my legs black and blue, just violent as hell." Davis was able to do another spin recovery. Nothing happened.

At about 5000 feet Davis felt his only option was to bail out. When he reached for the red door handle and jerked it down, nothing happened. The door refused to come off. Davis beat on the door with his hands, arms and elbows. Still, nothing happened. Davis was out of options, and hurtling nearer to the ground every second. He might have time for one more spin recovery. It was his only chance.

"This time," recalls Davis, "I went more slowly through the recovery procedures, trying not to panic. I eased the throttle all the way back, and I began to suspect at that time that the throttle may not have been all the back during my other attempts. Sure enough, I began coming out. Even though I was close to the ground, I waited and waited until I reached 150mph before I pulled up. I needed that much speed in order to avoid a secondary stall. I think I came to 200 or 300 feet above the ground."

As Davis leveled out, his body began to shake. He felt the trembling coming on and quickly trimmed the airplane, because he knew he wouldn't be able to fly it. After a minute or so his trembling subsided, he regained control of himself, and successfully landed the airplane.

On another occasion Davis and two other P-39 pilots flew from Portland to Longview, Washington which was situated by the beautiful Columbia River. Gracefully stretching across the Columbia was a bridge. The bridge seemed just high enough over the river to tempt the three P-39 pilots to attempt to fly under it—which they did.

After their P-39 training, the boys of the 354th Fighter Group boarded a train for Camp Kilmer in New Jersey. From there they boarded a French freighter for a trip to Europe. The ship was part of a convoy that according to Davis "stopped every ten minutes because of the sightings of German U–boats in the area. Three or four ships in the convoy ended up on the ocean's floor as the victims of the German submarines. After two and a half weeks at sea, Davis arrived in Reading, England where Col. Martin pointed to a sleek P-51 Mustang which had just landed and said, "That's it, that's what it's going to be fellows."

Davis was soon transferred to Boxted Field near Colechester, England. In order to get his flight time, Davis flew a British Spitfire. "It was a good airplane," recalls Davis, "but I didn't like sitting in the cockpit with my legs straight out in front of me; and you had to be careful in landing it." After 30 days at Boxted Field Davis flew his first combat mission. It was the very first time he had flown a P-51.

Davis' first mission was a flight over the English Channel into France flying P-51Bs. Along the way a few Me109s began attacking from below. Davis received word to drop his fuel tanks. Shortly after dropping his fuel tanks, his engine quit. He had already radioed that he was going down before it dawned on him that he had forgotten to switch to the Mustang's internal tanks. He switched to his internal tanks and the Mustang's engine roared to life. By then the flight had been broken-up and the Me109s had disappeared; and the flight was ordered to return to base.

On his fourth mission Davis' squadron was attacked from the side by Me109s. Many of the German pilots were very good, and very experienced. The American pilots who were shooting these enemy planes out of the sky were experienced pilots, too. Most of the new guys just did not have the hardened experiences to hone their skills. Davis remembers that it was difficult to get on the tail of an enemy airplane. After being on an enemy's tail, he would head for the clouds, and there were many clouds most of the time, and disappear. Davis' P-51 fired four 50cal. (two in each wing) which were bore-sighted to converge at 300 feet. On this particular mission Davis was able to maneuver behind a Me109 and fire until the Me109's wing came off. "The guy never did see me," recalls Davis.

One of the next dog fights in which Davis was involved occurred when he was escorting bombers. Davis sighted a Me109 positioning itself behind a box of bombers. The Me109 was quite far away, but Davis thought he could at least get close enough to fire and scare the enemy plane away. Davis fired from a distance and noticed that the Me109 had received some hits. The Me109 broke left into a dive, and remained in the dive until it hit the ground and exploded. Davis didn't see a parachute and assumed that the pilot was killed from the P-51's guns.

The AAF (Army Air Force) listed certain criteria to be met before a pilot was accredited with a kill. For example, the gun cameras had to show the enemy aircraft explode, break apart, a pilot bailing out, an actual crash, or two witnesses. Sometimes it was difficult to find two witnesses. A wingman, if in place, was a good witness, but that was only one. Many times during the melee of a dogfight, pilots were too busy with their own problems to notice what was going on around them; and sometimes at high altitude, gun cameras would freeze.

On a rare occasion, guns would also freeze. During a mission to Berlin, Davis got into a scrap and was able to maneuver behind a Me109. When he fired, however, only one of his four guns fired. Later, a motor was installed in the gun compartment which would help move the ammunition belt into the gun. Even though the Mustang had a two stage blower, it, like most planes, was not built to fight near the specified ceiling of its limit.

Davis recalls a mission on which his squadron got into a fight, and he was able to down a Fw190. After the fight, he found himself alone and was searching for his compass heading toward home when he spotted a silver, lone B-17, also on the way home, which was under attack by two Me109s.

Davis dived toward the two Messerschmitts. The three aircraft went around each other for a few minutes before the two enemy airplanes left the area. Davis was low on fuel and ammunition and knew that giving chase would not be a wise decision. He stayed with the B-17 until he reached the English Channel, then veered off and headed toward his base. The next evening, Davis was granted a three day pass and obtained a room at the Park Lane Hotel in London. The Park Lane was a "watering hole" for American military personnel, especially pilots. While waiting for a friend who was a P-38 pilot, Davis, who was enjoying a drink in the bar that night, was sitting next to two pilots. After some conversation, Davis discovered that the two men were the pilot and the copilot of the B-17 that he had befriended the day before. According to Davis, "I never had to buy myself a drink the rest of the evening."

After D-Day, Davis as a member of a flight of four P-51s, was flying patrols over the beaches. Suddenly, out of a slight overcast, about twenty Me109s dropped down behind them. We were all over the place and I hit a Messerschmitt so bad that his tail almost fell off.

"Then I spotted another Me109 close to the deck heading home," recalls Davis, "and I nosed over to follow him down. I think he must have been a new pilot. He was flying under power lines, thinking that I might hit one of them. I just nosed up and over the power lines. One airplane in my flight came down and fired at him and then flew away. I kept on the chase. The German pilot finally just bellied his plane to a landing; then climbed out on his wing and started waving at me."

Davis wanted to destroy the downed aircraft. He made a couple of circles attempting the best he could to chase the pilot away from the plane. Davis even made a pass and fired over the German pilot's head. The pilot wouldn't move. Davis made a low pass over the Me109 and opened fire. The Me109 blew up; and the pilot along with it.

"I have thought about that incident many times since then; and I still think of it sometimes," says Davis. "But it was war."

According to Davis, "There are three different counts on aircraft I shot down. The official kills recorded by the AAF are four. The officially acknowledged count by the AAF of five and a half, was not credited to him. When I went back to the states, unlike many pilots, I did not return to the squadron to pursue official credit for my claims. Some guy claimed a half of one of my kills; and that was strange, because I never saw another allied airplane in the sky. The third count is **my** count; it's in my head, and it is six and a half. But, it doesn't make any difference now—it's all over."

Regarding dog fighting, Davis reminisced, "I don't know whether I had the killer instinct in me or not. I wasn't real aggressive. I seemed always to fire before I was within the *killing range*."

While escorting bombers, we were told not to go below 2000 feet to chase enemy aircraft because it left the bombers vulnerable. I pretty much adhered to that policy. Many pilots who did chase to the ground usually registered more kills. The facts show that 80 percent of aircraft kills were made by those who closed in at close range."

Davis liked flying, and admits he had a good time. He didn't, however, like taking off in pairs of two into fog or rain and clouds. Sometimes they touched wing tips. To Davis, it was scary.

As far as navigation, before a mission the pilots were given the escort rendezvous time with the bombers, and the compass heading back home, which they wrote on the backs of their hands. Radio communication, other than with their fellow pilots while in the air, to the base or land was rare.

Returning to the United States, Davis was assigned to Kingman AFB base in Arizona where he taught combat flying, but other than that he didn't have much to do. On one flight in a P-63, the airplane would not reach full power on takeoff. He was able to keep it in the air and climbed to about 400 feet. He wanted to land as soon as possible. When the tower asked him if he desired a wheels-up landing, he answered that he wasn't sure what he wanted to do. He put the nose down and struggled to maintain some speed. Davis was a little shaken, but landed safely.

After landing and opening the cockpit, the crew chief of the P-63 jumped up onto the wing of the airplane and asked Davis, "What's the matter with you, don't you know how to fly an airplane?" Davis jumped out onto the wing and hit the crew chief so hard in the mouth that he fell completely off of the wing onto the ground. Davis worried about that incident because of the disciplinary action that could be taken against him—but nothing came of the incident, and the crew chief later apologized.

On another occasion, he and another pilot buzzed a car on a road which was heading toward the Grand Canyon. They were so low that the driver of the car panicked and ran off of the road. The driver was an AAF colonel, but luckily did not get their tail numbers, and nothing happened. But Davis, and his partner in crime, sweat that one out for awhile, too. While there, Davis was able to log some flying hours in P-47s.

Davis completed 68 combat missions with over 250 combat hours. The 354th Group unofficially counted 971 kills, and was awarded two Presidential Citations.

Davis was released from active duty in 1945 and entered college. Three years later he joined the reserves and retired as a Lt. Colonel.

Davis lives in Overland Park, Kansas with, Betty Jo, his wife of many years. They have three children: Guy, Gail and Clark.

RIGHT: Newly minted. AAF pilot Bill Davis

BELOW: A P-39 Airacobra in Portland

Davis and his crew chief, Dick Herman. The first P-51 to fly 50 missions.

The 354th Fighter Group celebrates its 500th kill. Davis is on the far right with a cigar in his mouth.

Article from a 1944 Topeka Capitol Daily

Davis' P-51, *Sport*.

Lt. William Davis Downs 5½ Nazis to Become Ace

Topekan on Third Mustang Named for Bird Dogs, 'Sport'

Chapter 14

Vernon Davy
Sailor

Background

Vernon Davy was born and raised in Michigan where his father was employed by the Postum Company. Vern was one of a family of four children; two boys and two girls. Vern and his brother, Bob, who was only 18 months older, enjoyed a very close relationship throughout their lifetime.

Davy enjoyed a happy childhood. Some of his fondest memories are of the summers he and his brother spent on their grandparents' farm near Petoskey, Michigan. The 120 acre farm, which was surrounded by the Hardwood State Forrest, was the perfect setting for young boys to roam and explore. Natural spring water ran freely, and deer and bears were not uncommon sights. The two boys rode horses, picked blackberries, picnicked and used their grandfather's old Model T for an army truck.

On Friday evenings they would travel to a small town and watch the free movies which were projected against the outside wall of *a filling station*. As the years flew by, they learned to cultivate the gardens and to tie the wheat left by the reaper during the wheat harvest into bundles. Later during his life Davy owned part of the farm.

When Davy was 15 years old his environment changed when his father, who held a degree in engineering, was transferred to Windsor, Ontario, Canada to assume the position of assistant general manager for the Post Cereal Plant.

During 1939 the war-clouds were settling in over Europe, and Canada required all boys to belong to the Canadian Cadet Corps.

Even though Davy and his brother, Bob, were American citizens, Bob talked Davy into joining. Bob became a lt. colonel and Davy became a sergeant major.

In 1942 when Davy's father secured a job with the Vickers Corporation making hydraulic pumps for B-29s, the family returned to Detroit.

Davy and Bob enjoyed making model airplanes. Since Bob was so captivated by airplanes, Davy decided he would travel a different path and became involved in ships and ship model making.

By 1942 the United States was involved in a world war, and Davy and Bob realized that it was only a matter of time before they would be called upon to help defend their country. Both boys wanted to receive their high school diplomas before they went into the service, so they knuckled-down and became honor roll students.

Davy joins the US Navy

Bob volunteered for the navy's V-5 program. He ended up flying TBMs off the USS *Princeton,* (CV37) in the Pacific, and retired as a lt. commander.

Davy was drafted into the US Navy in 1943 and sent to the Great Lakes Naval Training Center. After attending electrician school, Davy completed LCT (landing craft tanks) training at the Solomon's Island Maryland Amphibious Base.

After training, Davy boarded the Liberty Ship SS *Benjamin* in New York. His unit's LCT was on board the *Benjamin,* but in three pieces. Passing through the Panama Canal, and across the Pacific without convoy, they arrived in Milmey Bay, New Guinea where they assembled their (LCT 1137). They sailed up the coast and reached, what was to be their base of operation, Hollandia, in September 1944. Working from there, they supplied the US and Australian Armies on shore at Woendi and Atapi beachheads by offloading supplies from ships, and then taking them ashore.

According to Davy, "New Guinea is one of the most beautiful, and miserable, places on earth. The temperature was 120 degrees during the day and 100 degrees humidity all the time. There was copious amounts of rain. All of my personal gear mildewed."

Life at sea

Life on the LCT was primitive. Davy slept on a slung bunk with a two inch mattress and one of the world's renowned white navy blankets. A 16 inch fan at each end of the quarters provided the *air-conditioning*. A very small locker provided a place to stow their personal gear.

The LCT's menu was simple. It consisted of dried eggs, milk, rolls, bread and all the spam they could eat. When Davy's ship delivered beer ashore, the order always seemed to be a few cases short when it arrived at its destination. Davy's special assignment was to make certain that the LCT's refrigerator never broke down.

Davy's jobs during combat were to operate the anchor wench, and to man the twin 50 caliber machines on board. It seems that Davy was the only man on board who could fire the guns for a longer period of time without burning them up. Davy's promised tools never did arrive in Hollandia, so he confiscated what he could, and even had some sent to him from home. Davy not only acted as gunner, he also was the electrician, machinist assistant in the engine room, cleaned sand traps and changed oil in the engines.

Davy was respected by the skipper, and the crew of his ship for his resourcefulness and his innovations. One irritating problem on board was always having to hand-pump to obtain water. Davy scrounged an old bilge pump and hooked up water proof switches at each end of the hand pumps. It worked beautifully.

Another problem was that it took five and a half hours to change the oil in the ship's five engines. Actually, an old beer can was used to drain the oil of each crank case. Davy studied the ship's *Plan Book* and devised a method by which a pipe could be run from the engines to the bilge pump system, which would then suck the oil from the engines.

After the renovation, Davy's ship changed the engines' oil during a convoy in 30 minutes. It wasn't long before the convoy's flotilla engineering officer boarded Davy's ship demanding to know why his ship did not change oil during convoy. After Vern and his skipper showed their innovation to the engineering officer, the officer ordered the system installed on all LCTs.

On another occasion when Davy had a problem with the anchor winch shorting out from moisture, he installed a 200 watt lamp in the engine hood. Presto! The problem was solved. The commander ordered all LCT electricians to install the same system.

From Hollandia, number 1137 proceeded to the Philippines. Stopping for a few nights at Biak along the way, a Japanese aircraft which they called "washing machine Charlie" flew over every night and dropped a bomb. "He never seemed to hit anything," recalls Davy.

From Biak, Davy's ship traveled to Leyte and Samara Islands, where they refueled while under a full scale air attack. While proceeding through the Japanese held islands to Subic Bay where they were to load up for the Manila Bay invasion, they were escorted by P-38s during the day and P-61 *Black Widows* by night.

Because of a severe case of *jungle rot* Vern was removed from his ship and sent to a hospital in Manila. "There was shooting all around us," remembers Davy. The next day as Davy was evacuated in an ambulance to a hospital ship, his ambulance was peppered by sniper fire. One bullet entered the vehicle not too far above him as he lay on his back in the rear.

Fortunately, the army ambulance and its occupants arrived safely on a Manila beach, and Davy was carried aboard the hospital ship *Emily H. M Weder*. The *Weder* was a 522 foot ship that was built in 1920, had sailed in most parts of the world, and last served as a troop carrier under the name of *President Buchanan.*

The *Weder* transported Davy to a hospital in Hollandia where he resided for two weeks. After complete recovery, he was placed on an army troop ship and delivered back to Manila where he rejoined his ship.

From Manila Davy's ship sailed to Subic Bay, Philippines where the crew assisted in building a submarine base, and prepared for the invasion of the Japanese homeland. While at Subic Bay, Davy recalls the day, "I was on watch and I heard a lot of small arms fire. All our crew was ashore but me. Finally a guy came running down the beach hollering that the war was over. Soon I was relieved of watch and sent to the Group Command LCT where we celebrated by drinking warm beer."

On September 2nd, LCT 1137 departed Subic Bay, and seven days later dropped anchor off Okinawa long enough to load engineering equipment for Japan. Just past Ie Shima LCT 1137 was hit by a horrendous typhoon. "We rode it out at Unten Koo," remembers Davy, "We ended up 100 feet upon the beach." Miraculously, neither ship nor men suffered damage; but the ship had to be wrenched from the beach by two bulldozers and an LCM.

The landing on the beach at Wakayama, Japan was peaceful and lacked the stress of combat. However, what Davy observed during that landing gave him a reverent, thankful, pause for reflection. According to Davy, "I'm glad it was peacetime otherwise I don't think we would have survived our landing because we had to pass through three mine fields (which were cleared for us by the Japanese), sandbars, and land on a beach which had a cliff full of caves filled with artillery overlooking us." Historians have verified Davy's assessment of the situation; he would most assuredly have not survived. Davy has expressed the opinion of thousands of Americans when he stated, "I have to thank the A-Bomb for saving my life."

LCT 1137 operated as a ferry service between the Kuri Naval Base and the Eta Jima Hospital until February 1945, after which time the crew was ordered to Yokuska, Japan, where in April, they were decommissioned. The same month Davy boarded the *USS A.E. Anderson* and was shipped to San Francisco. The faithful LCT 1137 was left behind in Japan. On May 8th Davy received his discharge from the US Navy.

Civilian life

Once back home, Davy spent a year and a half at Wayne State College, but dropped out to attend a Radio-TV school. While there, Vern's friend introduced him to a neighbor girl named Fran. Fran swept the ex-sailor off his feet and soon they conjured up plans to marry in September 1950.

The US Navy calls again

In the meantime, Davy had joined the naval reserve. Davy's brother, Bob, talked Davy into transferring to the Naval Air Reserve. Davy transferred to Navy Squadron VA 732 in Grosse Ile, Michigan; the same squadron in which his brother served. Davy changed his rating to aviation electrician. Bob taught Davy to fly the navy's SNJ (AT-6), and Davy loved it.

The invasion of South Korea by North Korea in June 1950 altered Davy's life dramatically. Because of the need for the United States to rebuild its armed forces, Davy's naval reserve unit was recalled to active duty: and he and Fran married in August, a month earlier than planned. Davy railed to Moffet Naval Air Station in California before traveling by air to Barbers Point NAS in Hawaii. At Pearl Harbor he bordered the *USS Missouri BB 63*. The *Mighty Mo* sailed to Sasebo, Japan where he transferred to the *USS Graifia,* and later to the *USS Jason* which deposited him on the Sea Plane Tender *USS Curtis* at Iwakuni, Japan. On the way, however, the *Missouri* bombarded the coasts of Samchok and Pusan in Korea.

During January 195 I the *Curtis* departed Yokuska, Japan for Hunters Point, California to load atomic bombs (and hydrogen bomb detonators) and return to Eniwetok Atoll for experiments. Within approximately four months after returning to Eniwetok, Davy returned on the *Curtis* to San Diego where he was transferred to a hunter-killer antisubmarine squadron (VS 93 I) at Los Alamedas NAS. Fran met Davy in San Diego and accompanied him to his new assignment. Fran remained with him for the next six or seven months until he received his discharge in December of 1951.

Civilian life at last

Fran and Davy boarded a TWA Constellation for Detroit where Davy attended TV school. He enjoyed the work and subsequently worked in TV in Bay City, Michigan and later was employed as a service engineer for a welding machine company.

Davy and Fran built a comfortable living for themselves and their three children, Richard, Cricket and Kim. They had their own home and enjoyed time with friends at a cottage on Saginaw Bay.

After losing his job in Bay City, Davy moved to Kansas City, Missouri where he worked as an electrician for the Owens Corning Fiber Glass company for seven years before landing a job with TW A, where he remained for eighteen years.

Davy's family settled in Prairie Village and spent many good times camping, water skiing, cooking out and enjoying the Missouri Ozarks. Both Davy and Fran were certified scuba divers. Along the way, however, the family suffered a heart breaking tragedy with the death of daughter, Cricket.

Davy and Fran traveled to England, Scotland, Ireland, Portugal, Mexico, Alaska, Egypt, Greek Islands, cruised the Caribbean and scuba dived in the Bahamas and Nassau.

BELOW: Vern Davy in 1946.

BELOW: Vern's LCT offloading ashore.

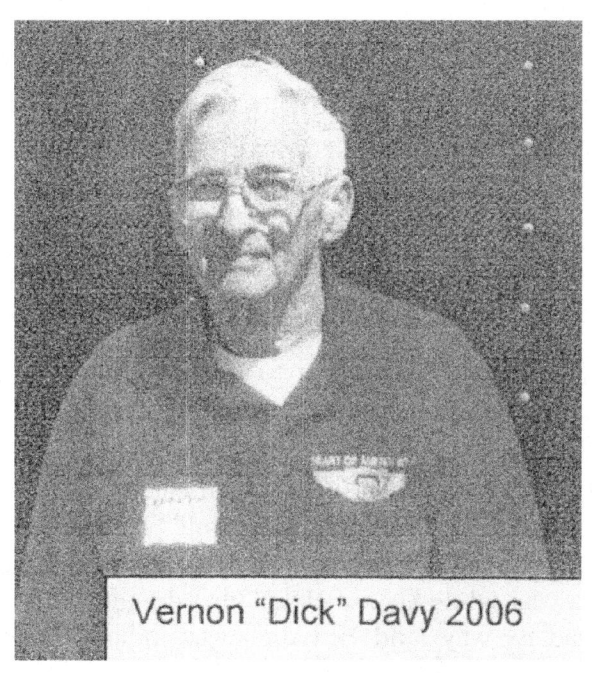
Vernon "Dick" Davy 2006

Chapter 15

Dan Fedynich
B-17 Ball Gunner

Background

As a boy growing up in Newark, New Jersey, Dan Fedynich (pronounced Fe-den-ich) was intrigued by airplanes, and spent many hours constructing models. His goal was to become an aircraft mechanic. Following his dream, Fedynich enrolled in a vocational school and had completed a year and a half of study toward an airframe and power plant certification when Uncle Sam pointed that famous finger at him saying, "I Want You."

Uncle Sam wanted Fedynich so badly that he wouldn't defer him even for a year while he completed his schooling. Thus, the draft board had its way, and Fedynich was inducted into the service on February 25, 1943 when he was 18 years old.

Once in the grip of the USAAF, Fedynich didn't spend very much time in one place. He started out at Fort Dix, New Jersey for induction training, then to Miami Beach, Florida for six weeks of basic, and later on to Lincoln, Nebraska for 16 weeks of power plant instruction on fighter type aircraft. Upon completion of training in Lincoln, Fedynich was sent to Burbank, California for five weeks of instruction on B-17s.

As is well known, the military works in strange ways. Since the AAF needed to fill the aerial gunners' positions in the rapidly produced bombers being sent to the ETO (European Theater of Operations), Fedynich was designated a gunner.

Hence, after his training in Burbank, he was sent to gunnery school in Las Vegas, Nevada.

Fedynich eventually was deposited in Tampa Park, Florida where he was assigned to a crew which conducted their transition training at nearby Drew Field. It was there that the crew got to know one another and learned to operate as a unit.

Destination England

After transition training, the crew picked up a brand new B-17G in Georgia and received orders to deliver it to the United Kingdom. After navigating their way along the standard route of Maine, New Hampshire, New Foundland and Scotland like the many crews who preceded them, they arrived in Deenthorpe, England. At Deenthorpe, where the crew was forced to relinquish their new B-17G, they were assigned to the Eight Air Force, 401st Bomb Group, 613th Bomb Squadron.

Fedynich was assigned the position of ball turret gunner. It is no secret that the ball turret positions on the B-17s and the B-24s were assignments not for the *faint-of heart*. On takeoff, the crewmen in the aft section of the Flying Fortress, the radioman and the gunners, would sit on the floor of the airplane in the radio shack until the aircraft was airborne.

As soon as the ammunition and bomb laden, jeopardous bomber perforated the clouds, Fedynich cranked the turret down from, and out, of the aircraft with the guns pointed straight down. When the guns were pointed down, the small door to the turret was positioned on top. Fedynich then opened the small door and squeezed himself inside. He stayed there until the Fortress began its decent for landing on the return from the mission.

When asked how he felt about his ball turret assignment, Fedynich, after laughing, replied, "Well, if one had claustrophobia, you wouldn't even get in there. I would say that, riding the ball, was kind of sticking your neck out. I never had any trouble with it; but we were only 18 years old, and most of us didn't have much fear then."

On one occasion Fedynich was in the ball turret of an older model B-17 which did not have a relief tube. So when he entered the ball, he took with him a small empty bomb fuse casing that had a screw-on lid. Somewhere over Germany at 28,000 feet with a temperature of 40 degrees below, he relieved himself into the casing, and replaced the lid. Soon, even with his electric suit turned up, the upper part of his body was freezing. He discovered that when he had moved his guns down, the urine had seeped from the unsecured lid of the casing and had, literally, frozen his back to the door. "As we neared the coast and began our decent," recalls Fedynich, "it melted and I was o.k. But if I had needed to bailout during the mission, I would have been out of luck." Fedynich occupied the ball turret position during all of his 33 missions.

Air Combat

Among Fedynich's targets were; Munich (3), Mossberg, Berlin, Inland, Edinburg, Weimer, Leipzig, Augsburg, Strasburg and Peen Mundey, Germany, which was a research facility for the V-I rocket.

"Fighter protection on most missions was pretty scant," recalls Fedynich. "We were just too slow. But, we would see some at different times. They would come and go. Many times we didn't know they were around." The predominant American fighter was the P-51. Sometimes they would see some P-47s. Most of the German fighters were Me 109s, and some Fw 190s. "Generally, the German fighters would *hit and run,"* remembers Fedynich. "I have seen them fly through our formation, shoot a plane down, and continue on until they disappeared. However, we did not see them every day."

On a mission to Weimer, Germany, Fedynich's Group was attacked by a wave of Me 109s. "From my position, 1 could see the massive formation lining up like a solid wall on the group behind us," says Fedynich. "I could see the flashes of 20 mm, and I knew they were under attack. I knew that we were next."
Soon, the 109s were racing toward Fedynich's formation at the six o'clock position. Fedynich's tail gunner poured a deadly stream of fire into an Me 109 right behind the tail of the B-17. "The prop stopped, and the canopy flew off," relates Fedynich, "and down he went."

Another Me 109 barrel-rolled right underneath Fedynich's ball turret. Fedynich pointed his twin 50s (armor piercing) downward and unleashed their power to the enemy. According to Fedynich, "I saw my ammunition hitting his wings, and he stalled out and fell toward the ground. I couldn't follow him all the way down because we were still under attack and I had to watch for other planes." Neither of the Me 109s were confirmed by anyone, nor did the gunners have gun cameras, so the kills were not credited to the gunners. Fortunately, all of the guns on Fedynich's Fortress always worked well. "We always test-fired our guns once we climbed to altitude over the sea," said Fedynich. "We never had gun jamming problems."

"One of the most dangerous things that really put a scare into me," recalls Fedynich, "was a perimeter crash we had." Fedynich and his crew were lined up for take off in an older model B-17. The aircraft was preparing for a long trip deep into Germany, and carried a full load of bombs and 2,780 gallons of fuel. As Fedynich's aircraft taxied down the perimeter behind the other slow moving aircraft in front of them, the brakes on Fedynich's Fortress went out.

The pilot made one of the only decisions available. He pulled the throttles on the left engines in an attempt to accelerate, and ground loop his aircraft in order to avoid smashing into the airplanes in front of him in the line. But, he was not fast enough, and the B-17 hit the aircraft in front of it.

The right wing of Fedynich's Fortress "tore into the tail of the airplane in front of us," recalls Fedynich, "and just destroyed the tail gun position." Fedynich's B-17 was tilted, as it lay motionless on the perimeter, and fuel was out pouring all over the airplane. "I was afraid of an explosion" recalls Fedynich. "We were sitting in the radio room when the top turret gunner ran up to us and told us to get out; and get out fast. We barreled out of that thing as fast as we could and ran as far as we could and then hit the deck and waited for the explosion. With all of that fuel, it would have taken only a little spark to set it off. Fortunately, no one was hurt. "But the crew still had the shakes when it was over," said Fedyinch. "We knew what could have happened."

Return Stateside

Fedynich's crew knew each other well, and they were close. Since the war, Fedynich has made several trips to visit his pilot who lives in Sikeston, Missouri, and his top turret gunner who lives in South Carolina. He contacted his copilot, who lives in California by phone. His navigator, who was later assigned to B-52s, lost his life from a failed parachute when he bailed out of a B-52.

When Fedynich returned to the United States after his service in Europe, the USAAF told him that they no longer need gunners; that they had plenty of airplanes and pilots in the Pacific theater. Thus, Fedynich was assigned to a factory school for C-54 transports at Douglass Aircraft Company in California. While working in the engine-build-up department at Travis AFB on C-54s with Air Transport Command, he volunteered for overseas duty. He was accepted, but the military would not reveal his destination.

After a very long flight from California, Fedynich was deposited at the remote Kadena Field on Okinawa. After thirty days on Okinawa, he volunteered to go to Dacca, India, where he was, again, assigned to C-54s, some of which were flying the *Hump* into China. By this time Fedynich had amassed enough points for discharge He left India and eventually arrived in Newark, New Jersey where he received his discharge on November 22, 1945.

In February of 1946 he went to work for TWA in the International Division in Newark, New Jersey. One of the several schools which Fedynich attended for TWA was in England. It was the only time that he ever returned. "It was the same old England" said Fedynich. "I never did care much for it, especially the food. I saw all of it I ever wanted to see." With the merger of TWA's International and Domestic Divisions, and because of Fedynich's special knowledge of props, he was transferred to Kansas City, Missouri.

In 1950, during the early stages of the conflict in Korea and the build up of the American military, Fedynich, who had been in the inactive air force reserve since 1945, was recalled into the USAF.

He was sent to Keesler Air Fore Base in Biloxi, Mississippi where he was assigned to the Reclamation Department. His first project was tearing down four B-29s to be used for aluminum scrap. Eventually he was assigned as an aircraft inspector for Beechcraft C-45s. In 1951, after a year at Keesler Air Force Base, Fedynich was released from the military and returned to TWA and Kansas City.

Civilian Life

Fedynich spent 46 years with TWA. For 12 years he was a mechanic, and later became a lead mechanic (now called *crew chief)* for 14 years. For the last 20 years Fedynich was a supervisor.

Fedynich flew 33 combat missions with the 8th Air Force. For his service to our country, he was awarded the American Theater Ribbon; European-African-Middle Eastern Ribbon with 3 Bronze Stars; Air Medal with 3 Bronze Oak Leaf Clusters; Distinguished Flying Cross and the World War II Victory Medal.

Fedynich still carries a high interest in airplanes. That's one of the reasons he joined the CAF, Heart of America Wing. When offered a chance to fly in our HOA war birds, Fedynich declined. "I have all the respect and confidence in the world in our Wing's pilots," said Fedynich. "But airplanes are made up of parts, and I have seen enough of those to make me shy away from flying for now."

Dan Fedynich's wife, Vanita, now deceased, operated their 80 acre farm on which they lived in Kansas City, Kansas. He and Vanita had two sons.

Below: The B-17, Homing Pigeon, which Fedynich flew in over Nazi Germany.

Fedynich 1944

Fedynich 2007

Chapter 16

Sally Hatch
WWII British Soldier

Childhood

As 14 year old Sally Hatch was riding her bicycle back to her home from visiting her older sister, she became acutely aware that a low flying airplane was heading straight toward her. She thought at the time that it was a strange looking aircraft. Suddenly, the nose of the airplane moved downward, and the war machine was pointed directly toward young Sally. She saw, and heard, the bursts of the deadly machine gun fire as it raged toward her. She threw her bike down, and as the bullets kicked up dirt from the narrow lane, Sally ran into the woods and tried to conceal herself behind the trees.

The German warplane executed only one low pass, pulled up and continued to fly on. Shortly afterward Sally heard the explosions of bombs. She learned later that planes had attacked a submarine factory nearby which took the lives of 40 people. Sally recovered her bike and continued her journey home.

There was a military barracks near her town, and one would have expected the German plane to strafe roads by the compound. However, there were no soldiers around when the airplane tried to gun down Sally. Sally believes that the pilot may have thought that she was a soldier.

Sally was the middle child of seven children and lived with her family in Norwich, England. Norwich was a medieval town of unequalled greatness, and renowned for its 900 year old Norman Cathedral. It is located on the River Wensum about 18 miles from the North Sea, and about 115 miles northeast of London. In 1940 about 126,000 people were listed as citizens of the agricultural fertile town.

Since the end of WWII, stories and movies have appeared which tell about spies who tried to communicate with the Germans off the coast; and how German submarines would quietly unload soldiers near land so that they could sneak ashore. Sally recalls one incident where a German landing party reached the shores. As she recalls the incident, however, she believes that they were all soon rounded-up. Since Sally had begun her schooling at age four, she had graduated by the time she turned fourteen. Once out of school Sally entered a seven year lithograph apprentice program.

Sally was not making a lot of money in the apprentice program. Consequently, at the urging of many of her friends, she quit the program and went to work in a factory which paid more money. "But," recalls Sally, "I hated that job."

War had been thrust upon Great Britain in 1939. Sally had seen her friends and relatives heed the call of the bugle and march off to war. "The war will be over," thought Sally, "before I can do anything for my King or my country." At age 15, and with out informing her parents, Sally joined the army.

Hatch joins the army

British law dictated that one could join the military at age 17 and a half, if they were granted parental consent. Sally was disqualified on both points.

When Sally reached age 16 and a half she went to the military station and enlisted again. She lied about her age. When it came time for the army to obtain parental consent, Sally's mother was against it. But Sally's father, who had served in WWI, finally said, "If that's what she wants to do, let her do it." Her parents signed the papers. Sally was a British soldier. There was one unresolved problem, however; the army thought she was 17 and a half. Sally had lied, and gotten away with it

When the authorities asked Sally what she wanted to do in the army, Sally told them that she wanted to be in the signal corps as a wireless (English term for radio) operator. Within a short period of time, Sally was sent to northern England for a three months training course, part of which was learning the Morse code.

This was the first time that Sally had been away from home. Her training location was 150 miles from Norwich (which was considered quite a distance in 1940s England). Sally was from a large, close-knit family. Even though she loved her wireless operators' program, her stomach felt the pangs of homesickness. After completing her three month training course, 16 year old Sally happily headed home on a seven day leave.

After reporting back to duty Sally was assigned to a heavy artillery unit as a radio operator at a command post. The command post was a huge dug-out about six feet into the ground. Inside the dug-out were maps, radios and plotting tables. The purpose of the unit was to track the incoming German aircraft and shoot as many out of the sky as possible. Sally's command post was near the center of England at a place called Stockton on-Tees.

She took courses in *aircraft spotting,* and like most Britons, could recognize both enemy and allied aircraft. She could spot an Me 109, Fw 190, the inverted gull wing of the Stuka as well as she could her countries' Spitfire fighter and Lancaster bomber. Sally's job was to go down into the dugout command post and deliver the communications from the headquarters unit to the plotters so they would know how to position the powerful 4.6 mm. guns. She was to identify the kinds of aircraft (pictures of which were pinned to the walls of the bunkers) and tell the plotters what kind of aircraft were headed their way as she handed them her messages.

Sally had been in the army for about six months before she went home on leave again. While she was home, she enjoyed her 17th birthday. "I felt a little bit quilty about lying to the army about my age," recalls Sally. "So when I got back to my duty station I asked to speak to my commanding officer." Sally told him that she had lied about her age. When the CO found that she was now 17, he told Sally that she could leave the military if she desired. But patriotism ran deep within Sally's heart and soul, and she declined the release.

The army wrote a letter to her parents and explained the conversations. The army communication related that they had spent a great deal of money training Sally, and that she was a good radio operator; therefore they would like to keep her if the parents did not object. Sally's parents did not object.

Shortly afterward Sally's 356th Heavy Artillery Battery was moved near Edinbrough, Scotland. While Sally was stationed in Scotland she met a man that was attached to the Royal Navy. Marion Keathley was an American who hailed from rural Sedalia, Missouri. Keathley had gone to Canada in the early1940s and enlisted in the Royal Canadian Air Force. He was later transferred and attached to the RAF, and by the time Sally met him he was attached to the navy. Within a year they were married.

While in Scotland Sally and ten other women were interviewed to take a job at the war office in London operating a hollirith machine. Even though the hollirith machine had nothing to do with the signal corps, Sally and the other young ladies remained attached to the signal corps.

The hollirith machine was similar to a present day computer. In brief, it was a coding machine that punched holes in cards to send and receive secret messages. Eventually these messages had to be filed away within the British war office. Sally loved punching secret messages in, but she hated the filing part of the job.

Working in London in 1943 was almost like being on the front lines. Sally observed thousands of German aircraft fly over London and reign bombs down on her beloved country. Most of the bombings were at dusk.

Some of Sally's watches consisted of standing outside the housing and barracks facilities to watch for enemy aircraft. In case of incendiary bombs, it was Sally's job to make certain that the other women were out of the housing units and into the underground shelters below.

On one of Sally's watches she heard a terribly loud groaning noise. She looked to the sky and saw so many aircraft that it just appeared to be a big black cloud. She knew soon that she would hear the horribly loud explosions, the whistling of the bombs, the sirens, and all of the other, sometimes unidentifiable, excruciating sounds of a raid. At about that time an officer came out and asked Sally, "Are you afraid?" Sally replied, "Yes, I am." The officer's retort was, "So am I."

Sally remembers that the bomb raids "were very scary." She confesses that every time she was in a bomb raid, the primary thought which ran through her mind was whether she would ever be able to see her family again.

Bombing raids

The air raids Sally experienced at her duty stations in the army were not foreign to her. The citizens of Norwich had begun building shelters, organizing and training for raids immediately after Germany's invasion of Poland on September 3, 1939. A total of 11 air raid sirens in Norwich sounded a total of 1,443 alerts over the last four years of the war. The senseless, indiscriminate bombing of the center of Norwich by the Germans was very destructive. All of the children carried gas masks to school with them.

Sally remembers being herded into the small shelters in her home town. "The sirens would go off every night," recalls Sally. "We spent most of the nights in the cellars. We had six bunk beds down there and mother would read to us. I always hated it. I felt trapped." The city helped build shelters for the residents. Many small brick shelters were built in the gardens. Some shelters, built of corrugated iron, were called Anderson shelters because they were introduced when Sir John Anderson was Home Secretary. However, the people used cupboards, tables, or anything they could find to use for cover.

After the war was over Sally's mother told her that she had purchased some poison, and that if she had seen the Germans coming toward their home, she would have poisoned all of her children.

The pamphlet, *Assault Upon Norwich, The Official Account of the Air Raids on the City,* by R.H. Mottram, and published by the Soman Wherry Press Ltd, Norwich, lists 340 killed and 1,432 citizens injured for the years 1940 through 1943. The account further states that almost 2,100 dwelling houses (residents' homes) were destroyed, over 2,600 seriously damaged and 25,621 moderately and slightly damaged. Since the dwelling houses census in 1939 Norwich totaled 35,569, according to *Assault Upon Norwich,* the figures indicate that 85 percent of the homes in Norwich were affected by the bombings.

Sally describes the German V-1 rockets as something you could see. "They always flew very low," remembers Sally. "Sometimes they were so low they were hard to shoot down with our artillery. As long as you could hear their loud motors you felt fairly safe. But when the motor stopped, and it became silent, it was time to take cover, because they would just fall straight down from the sky. The V-2s were faster and more controlled than the V1s, and most of them were headed toward London."

After her stint in London, Sally was transferred to Salisbury in 1944 to resume her work as a radio operator. According to Sally, "Not much was going on in Salisbury. There were Americans there and we helped them with their tanks and briefed them on the English weather." While at Salisbury, Sally married Keithley, and became a war bride.

Of the seven children in Sally's family, only she and her older brother, Ernest, served in the British military. Ernest, who was four years older than Sally, enlisted in the Royal Air Force (RAF). Ernest was trained as a pilot, but due to a serious back injury when he was trying to secure British Lancasters to the ground in a storm, he was removed from pilot status. He was, however, assigned to navigator duty on the renowned four engine Lancaster bomber.

Among Sally's files is a letter dated April 27, 1944 which was sent to Mrs. Hatch from the Wing Commander of number 106 Squadron, which reads in part:

> I am writing to express my sympathy…upon the receipt of the news that your son, Sergeant E.A. Hatch, is missing from operations…He was a gunner of an aircraft which left here on the night of 26th April 1944, to carry out a bombing raid on Schweinfurt…There is absolutely no knowledge of what happened and it can only be assumed that the aircraft was a victim of enemy fighters or ground defenses….

Sally did not receive much information about the crash. She didn't know any of the crew members who went down with her brother. Soon however, she learned that her brother perished and was buried in France.

Back to civilian life

Sally remained in the army for nine months after her marriage. In 1945 after Keithley had spent five years attached to the British military, he decided to return to the United States. He requested that the British discharge his wife so that she could return to America with him; and the British complied with his request.

Sally remembers how thrilling it was to arrive in the United States. "Everyone was so patriotic, and there were flags flying," recalls Sally. "My father was patriotic, too. I remember that he used to get very upset wondering when the United States was ever going to enter the war, including WWI." Sally is an international patriot. Tears come to her eyes when any country plays their national anthem.

There is a monument near Sally's home in Kansas that honors all American veterans (combat or not) from all of the American services. Every Veteran's Day she visits the memorial and sits down quietly on one of the concrete benches; and in silence she prays, and pays her respect to our servicemen.

Sally has many fond memories of her beloved England, where many of her relatives still reside, and has thought of returning there to live.

She remembers the war years well. It was a joyous day for the English people when Britain and her allies finally crushed the Axis powers, and the German *blitzkrieg* (lightening warfare) became a term confined to the history books.

According to Sally, "The thought that England would lose the war never entered my mind. I knew we would win." Sally's faith, however, was a mere echo of all of the English people. The steadfast belief that their nation would prevail was reflected in the song, *The White Cliffs of Dover*. The song was written by Nat Burton (words) and Walter Kent (melody), and made famous throughout the allied nations by singer Vera Lynn. For example:

There'll be blue birds over
The white cliffs of Dover
Tomorrow, just you wait and see.
...and there were...

And Jimmy will go to sleep,
In his own little room again.

...and he did, and so did a lot of little Sallys, too...

AFTERMATH

Sally Keithley had two children, a boy, Richard, and a girl, named Janet. She has nine grand children. After 41 years of marriage, Keithley died of leukemia. Five years later Sally married Jean McCulley. McCulley owned an oil company and he and Sally remained in Kansas. McCulley passed away in 2000.

Shortly after the war information about the crash of her brother's Lancaster slowly became known. For one thing, Sally learned that Ernest was buried with six of his crew in Bayard, France. Bayard, about 90 miles outside of Paris, was near the 1944 crash site. The family had talked about returning his body to England for reburial.

She learned, also, that one crewman survived the crash and was still living. It seems that no one was able to bail out of the aircraft on that fateful night. All were killed, probably upon impact, except the copilot, Roy Bradley.

When the Germans reached the downed aircraft, they counted the bodies and knew that one was missing. Bradley had fled the scene of the crash and was hidden in the village by the local citizens. When he was told by a villager that the Germans were lining up the town's inhabitants, and would shoot them one by one until they surrendered the downed airman, Bradley walked out and gave himself up. Bradley spent the rest of the war as a German POW.

In 1993 Sally began writing letters to the mayor and other officials in Bayard. She requested permission to visit the gravesite, conduct a small ceremony, and place an RAF flag on the graves of the seven airmen.

Sally knew that the French villagers had buried the seven crewmen side by side. She knew that they were buried in graves one to seven in the Laneuville-a-Bayard Churchyard. Since Sally had never been there, she politely asked the French officials if a villager or two could direct her to the grave site once she arrived.

In 1994 when Sally, her husband and two of her sisters from Norwich arrived in the French village, they were stunned. The whole town of Bayard, a French color guard, 20 or more dignitaries, and six young French pilots greeted them. The hugs and tears were plentiful, and she attended a four hour luncheon. She even talked with a few older citizens who had witnessed the blazing fire of the Lancaster that night.

The villagers knew Bradley, because every year he travels from his home in England to participate in the ceremony which honors the heroic airmen. The graves and the grounds of the cemetery are well kept, and flowers are abundant. Sally's brother, Ernest, is respectfully honored every year. The French people, young and old, are Ernest's friends in death. According to Sally, "I don't want his remains returned to England. I want him to stay right where he is. That is where he belongs."

BELOW: Sally in uniform in 1942. All photos from Sally Keathley-McCulley's files

BELOW: A 63 year old photograph showing 16 year old Sally Hatchin her British Army uniform. Because she lied about her age, the army thought she was 17 and a half.

BELOW: Sally's 3 bedroom home, built in 1929 in Norwich, England. Photo taken several years after the war.

Chapter 17

Albert C. Henke
B-17 Tail Gunner

Background

Albert C. Henke came into this world on a warm July day in Brunswick, Missouri. He was the middle sibling of an older brother and a younger sister. Before Henke reached his first birthday, his adventurous father packed up the family and moved to Ranger, Texas to seek his fortune in the burgeoning oil business. After a few years in Borger, Henke's father accepted a job in the wild and wooly town of Borger, Texas. Borger was a new bustling oil town out in the *middle of nowhere* located among the tumbleweeds. The rugged Texas Rangers finally settled things down some. But when Henke and his family first arrived, they set up housekeeping in a tent until the oil company finished building a house for them.

About 1928 Henke's father moved to Ponca City, Oklahoma. The Great Depression hit. The oil company went broke. Henke loaded his family of five, and all of their worldly possessions in a trailer, including his wife's Singer sewing machine, hooked it to his 1926 Model-T Ford, and headed back to Missouri where he settled in Kansas City.

Young Henke attended school in Kansas City, Missouri, and in the summer, worked on his uncle's farm. Young Henke was 13 years old when his father died. The family was destitute. Henke's mother took in ironing and cleaned houses. The four remaining members of the Henke family barely got by. Henke's older brother,

Harold, was able to get a job in Kansas City at the Western Auto Supply Company. Later, Harold was able to land Henke a job at Western Auto Supply Company, too. By pooling all of their financial resources, the Henke family prevailed.

A World War beckons

The Japanese bombing of Pearl Harbor on December 7, 1941, as it did for thousands of Americans, changed the lives of the Henke family. Brother Harold joined the United States Army Air Force in 1941. Young Henke joined the same branch a year later. Both boys felt that with their mother and sister working in their own café, along with the money they sent home, the family would get along.

Henke joined with his cousin, Roy Bates. The military promised them that they could remain together throughout their military career. That proved to be a promise unfulfilled. After a few days at Fort Leavenworth, Kansas, Henke was assigned to Midland, Texas for his basic training. Like most green recruits, Henke was trained under a sarcastic drill sergeant. In the typical Texas drawl, the sergeant told the trainees, "Aren't you lucky to be in this great state of Texas? You're in the army now. You can gripe all you want, but it won't do you any good." Every morning during calisthenics, the sergeant would shout, "Aren't you lucky to see this beautiful Texas sunrise?"

Near the end of his basic training, Henke decided to sign up for armament school with some of his new found friends. He was accepted and was sent to armament school at Buckley Field in Aurora, Colorado. Because of the need for aircraft gunners in Europe, the 15 week course was shaved down to nine weeks. Henke was trained to refer to his machine gun as a caliber .50 machine gun—not a .50 caliber machine gun. To this day, Henke becomes irritated when he reads, or hears, someone refer to a machine gun in any other way; which, of course, is most of the time.

During armament school Henke applied for aerial gunnery school. He passed all of the tests and graduated as an aerial gunner in May 1943. A month later, without ever receiving his promised furlough, Henke boarded the prewar luxury liner *USS Mariposa* and sailed to Casablanca, Morocco where he arrived on his 23rd birthday. During the voyage, his wallet and all of his money was stolen.

After a month at Casablanca, Henke boarded a railroad boxcar for a 1,200 mile, eight-day trip to Tunis, Tunisia. It was a miserable trip. The boxcar had run over a cow which was on the tracks, and the dead cow's terrible stench permeated the boxcar during the whole trip. At one point, because of the crowded boxcar, Henke was sleeping on top of the boxcar, when a friend awakened him just in time to climb down before his head was going to hit some power lines before entering a tunnel. At Tunis, Henke slept on the ground before some trucks transported him to his assigned air base at Oudina, Tunisia. Arriving at Oudina, Henke had to sleep on the ground for a few more nights (among lizards, snakes and various bugs) before he was assigned to a permanent tent.

Combat in the skies

All flyers, pilots and crewmen had to fly 50 combat missions before they could be rotated back to their beloved United States. Many of the airmen were killed, or taken prisoner before they ever completed their 50 missions. Some were killed during their first mission, others on their 50th mission. Knowing this, Henke volunteered right away for combat because he wanted to get it over as soon as possible and go home.

After a matter of days at Oudina, where Henke was assigned to the Fifteenth Air Force, 99th Bomb Group, 416th Squadron, he flew his first combat mission. He was assigned as a tail gunner on the renowned B-17 Flying Fortress which had the dubious name *Widow-Maker* painted on its nose. This would be Henke's very first time in a B-17. The mission, along with 144 other aircraft, was to bomb a bridge and railroad marshalling yard at Benevento, Italy. Henke's Flying Fortress was at the very end of the formation (known as tail-end Charlie), which was always vulnerable to being one of the first bombers to be shot down.

After finally finding the latch to release his guns from a locked position, he found the red knob to release oxygen into his mask. But he turned it on high, and felt a steady stream of full force air blowing in his face during the whole mission. The pilot, upon landing, wondered why the airplane's oxygen supply was so low. As Henke remarked, "It's a good thing it was a short mission."

It took the next six and a half months for Henke to complete his 50 missions. During that time he participated in bombing missions over the cities of Benevento, Viterbo, Pisa, Turin, Bolzano, Prato, Rome, Anzio, Cassino, Verona, Genoa and Verona in Italy; Maribor and Pola in Yugoslavia; Sifia, Bulgaria; Athens and Salonika in Greece; Steyr and Klagenfurt in Austria; and Regensburg, Germany.

He flew in the positions of waist gunner, ball turret and tail gunner. He flew in B-17s with nose art that read *Widow Maker, Bad Penny, Sweater Girl, Miss Peggy, Lady Luck, Smiley, Robert E. Lee, Spoofer* and *Fort Alamo II*.

On his sixth mission to Terni, Italy they bombed, and set many oil fires in the marshalling yards. It was the first mission where Henke's group was attacked by the deadly German Me-109s and Fw-190s fighter aircraft. Three of the planes flown by crack German pilots, were shot down. "What a rough day," remembers Henke. "This mission was one I will never forget. It was a relief to get back to the base." On his seventh mission he saw at close range one of the bombers in his squadron take a direct hit and go down blazing in flames.

On his ninth mission the tail gunner in the B-17 next to his was killed. On most of his missions, Henke's crew faced flak from the large enemy guns on the ground. Sometimes the flak was deadly accurate. Just before Henke's 13th mission he received his draft notice. He told his pilot that he couldn't go on the mission because he had to report to his draft board in Kansas City. His pilot suggested that Henke write his draft board and tell them, "Come and get me."

Near the end of 1943, Henke's 99th Bomb Group moved to an airfield in Foggia, Italy. According to Henke, his 36th mission was, "My roughest raid so far." In fact, the USAAF gave the airmen two missions credit for the raid. The purpose of the mission was to destroy aircraft factories in Regensburg, Germany. Flak and enemy fighters were fierce. Henke hit several enemy fighters with his twin caliber .50 machine guns, and shot one down. He saw several American planes on fire, and falling earthward.

Regensburg proved disastrous to the Americans, especially because of deadly German fighters. (See the clipping from the *Kansas City Star*).

Germany reported that 119 allied planes, including 95 four engine bombers, were shot down that day. Henke's crew was the only one of his squadron to return to the base.

Henke completed his 50th mission on April 2, 1944. It was a rough mission. His group was attacked off and on for over two hours by about 300 enemy aircraft. The flak was extremely thick. "We lost 51 bombers and destroyed 129 enemy fighters," recalls Henke.

During his six and a half months of combat, Henke observed 55 airplanes explode. Of the 800 gunnery students in his class, only 153 of them survived the war. Henke was one of them.

From warrior to civilian

Fifteen days after his last combat mission, Henke boarded a B-17 at his air base in Foggia, Italy and began the first leg of his trip back to the United States. Sailing home as part of a convoy, which encountered enemy submarines and a vicious storm at sea, Henke arrived in New York City in June of 1944. He finally received his military discharge on September 12, 1945.

It wasn't long before Henke went back to Western Auto Supply. His new position was a buyer in the Supply and Equipment Department. Henke's new secretary, a young woman named Mary Haas, from Shawnee, Kansas, caught Henke's eye, and then, his heart. They were married in September 1947. They had four children, Nancy, Marsha, Don and Sharon. After 41 continuous years at Western Auto Supply, Henke retired; but worked at the company another 19 years under the Senior Overload Program. He and Mary are still married and reside in Overland Park, Kansas.

The Army Air Force strongly suggested that airmen not keep diaries of their combat experiences. Henke, however, kept one anyway. He kept it hidden in the bottom of his shaving kit, and used it to publish a recent hardbound-cover book entitled, ***Adventures Under Fire***, *World War II Memoirs and 50-Mission Diary Aboard the B-17 Flying Fortress 1942 to 1945*. The book is packed with memorable stories, photographs and pages from his actual diary. It tells of his friendships with those who survived, and those heroes who lost their lives. The cost of the 288 page book is $29.95, and may be ordered by contacting Leathers Publishing at 1-888-888-7696, www.rainydaybooks.com., or e-mailing the Henke family at ACHenkeWWII@aol.com.

The following article appeared in the Kansas City Star on February 23, 1944 which told of the Regensburg raid.

FiERCE AIR FIGHT

U.S. Armadas from Britain and Italy Shoot Down 133 Nazi Fighters
APART ON YANK LOSS London Statement Says Toll Is 6\ Bombers, but Mediterranean Reports 53.

British Capital Takes a Heavy Jolt in eight, but Ten Craft Are Bagged.

London, Feb. 23, 1944 (AP)-American bombers and fighters, striking powerfully from Britain and Italy in the first coordinated assault deep into Germany, crippled enemy aircraft production anew and knocked 133 Nazi fighter planes from the sky, United States army headquarters declared today.

Sixty-one big bombers were lost in yesterday's joint assault, which included diversionary raids by planes based in Italy, the announcement said. It listed forty-one bombers lost from the force attacking from Britain, and twenty missing from the U.S. 15th air force based in Italy.

Differ on Figures.

(Allied headquarters in the Mediterranean said only fifteen Italy-based planes were lost yesterday, and a spokesman said twelve were bombers. This would make the day's total bomber losses fifty-three)
"In three days of record breaking operations aimed at destroying Germany's capacity to maintain aerial resistance, American air force planes have accounted for 310 enemy fighters," headquarters said, with 153 falling to fighters of the 8'h and 9'h air forces in Britain, 117 destroyed by 8'h air force bombers, and forty by 15,h air force bombers.

The Germans threw up savage resistance as the Britain-based bombers struck the Junkers-88 assembly plant at Bernburg and air-frame and component factories at Aschersieben and Halberstadt. The 15th air force bombers from Italy blasted two Messerschmitt factories at Regensburg and bombed freight yards at Petershausen, twenty miles north of Munich.

Fierce Sky Battles.

Heavy bombers flying from Britain bagged thirty-four enemy fighters yesterday, and their escorts knocked down fifty-nine, while the bombers of the 15'h air force destroyed forty Nazi craft.

South of Regensburg, Flying Fortresses engaged in a 55-minute battle with a score of ME-109s, ME-210s and FW-190s. Over the target, they were challenged by nine planes, and Staff Sgt. A. C. Henke, 8319 Morrell Avenue, Kansas City, tail gunner, who destroyed a ME-210, said:

"Jerry came in on a level.

I fired when he was way out, and stayed on the trigger. He finally broke away, smoking heavily, and fell beneath us."

A communiqué said that the 8'h and 9'h air forces lost eleven fighters yesterday, and that two fighters of the force in Italy were missing, for a total day's loss of seventy four planes.

Today's German communiqué asserted 119 Allied planes, including ninety-five 4-engined bombers, were destroyed yesterday over Germany.

Loss of sixty-one bombers over Germany Tuesday is a new record, since it is the first figure for combined operations from Britain and Italy of the United States strategic air force in Europe.

R.A.F. Mosquitoes maintained the offensive during the night, hitting unspecified targets in Western and Southwestern Germany without loss.

The following was enjoyed by the men stationed in Italy.

Italy: Hitch in Hell

I'm sitting here a thinkin' of what I left behind,
So I'll put it down in writin' what's runnin' through my mind.
We've dropped so many bloomin' bombs and done so many flights,
An' froze our feet an' hands an' things while at sub-zero heights.
But there is one consolation. Now you listen while I tell.
When we die, we'll go to heaven, cause we've done our hitch in hell.

We've taken a million Atabrine, those dirty yellow pills, To
fortify our systems agin' the fever an' the chills.
We've seen a million ack-ack bursts around us in the sky.

Fear gripped our hearts and chilled our blood when flak began to fly.
    "Put on those lovin' flak suits," we hear our pilots yell,
    "Cause this ain't a bloomin' picnic. It's another hitch in hell."

But when the taps have sounded, and we leave our earthly cares,
    We'll stage our best parade of all, upon the Golden Stairs.
    Angels will be there to meet us, and harps will softly play.
    We'll draw a million dollars, and we'll spend it in a day.
    Gabriel will be there to meet us, and St. Peter will proudly yell,
    "Front seats, you guys from Italy. You've done your hitch in hell."

by Lt. Harry R. Hathaway
Killed in Action, February 22, 1945
348th Bomb Squadron - 99th Bomb Group

ABOVE: Albert C. Henke.
BELOW: Henke in his high-altitude heat suit, oxygen mask & parachute.

Chapter 18

Earl W. McCabe
Marine Fighter Pilot

Discovering someone around the ole' neighborhood that has personally visited with the world renowned aviator, Charles A. Lindbergh, is, indeed, a rare occurrence. However, 85 year old Overland Park resident, Earl W. McCabe, is one of those rare individuals who has.

McCabe also holds the distinction of being befriended by one of America's most famous (sometimes defined as infamous) women aviators, "Poncho" Barnes; and of flying in combat with former members of "Pappy" Boyington's *Black Sheep* Squadron.

Marine Corps Fighter Pilot

After attending the Kansas City Junior College (which was located in downtown Kansas City, Missouri) for two years; McCabe, at age 19, joined the United States Navy Flight Training Program in 1942.

After training at Missouri Valley College in J-3 Piper Cubs, he completed more training in the Stearman biplane (Yellow Peril), the BT-13 (Vultee Vibrator), and the single engine, single float OS2U seaplane. The OS2U was designed to be catapulted from battleships. McCabe enjoyed flying the OS2U when landing and taking off from the sea, because of the long runways which the open expanse of water provided.

After receiving his *wings of gold*, Second Lieutenant McCabe was granted an assignment to Marine Fighter Squadron VMF-218 at Mojave Air Base in California flying Grumman F4F Wildcats.

Landing in "Poncho" Barnes' Back Yard

Barnes was a tough adventurer who counted among her drinking-buddies such notables as Howard Hughes, Tyrone Power, John Wayne and Chuck Yeager. She was an active stunt, test and racing pilot. Barnes was kind of a later-day Calamity Jane, only Barnes strapped an airplane to her waist rather than a gun belt. Barnes was depicted in the movie, The Right Stuff, as the owner of the Happy Bottom Riding Club drinking establishment near Edwards Air Force Base.

During 1943 McCabe and another pilot were refused requests for landing at Mojave because of deteriorating weather. They were diverted to Muroc Army Air Base (later named Edwards Air Force Base) about 20 miles away. Despite rain and strong winds, McCabe and his cohort planted their F4Fs on a short, sage brush filled runway, and taxied behind a hangar.

According to McCabe, "A woman with broad shoulders, who looked at first like a man, came toward us saying, 'That's alright, boys, I know your colonel. I'll call him and tell him you're here.'" After Barnes took them in her home, the walls of which were adorned with aviation trophies and photographs of her friends, including Amelia Earhart and Charles Lindbergh, she fed them and allowed them to sleep in her hangar overnight.

Black Sheep Territory

Eventually McCabe's squadron was assigned to Bougainville in the Solomon Islands where they flew the 450mph F4U Corsairs, and were quartered on an air base with "Pappy" Boyington's famed *Black Sheep* Squadron. McCabe arrived in December of 1943. A couple of months later Boyington was shot down by ground fire on a raid over Rabaul and captured by the Japanese. The *Black Sheep* Squadron was disbanded and five of the pilots joined McCabe's VMF-218; and McCabe flew with them on several occasions.

According to McCabe, "The Hollywood version of all of the pilots of the *Black Sheep* Squadron being *misfits* was not true; and I never saw any of those pretty nurses around, either."

Charles A Lindbergh Instructs VMF-218

"Charles Lindbergh had always been one of my heroes, even before I became a pilot," recalls McCabe. The first time McCabe met Lindbergh was at Mojave in 1943 when Lindbergh flew a lone 2,000hp F4U onto the field with the purpose of rendering the young flyers some valuable advice on flying the rugged Corsair. "It was exciting," remembers McCabe, "to see this tall, slim man in a gray suit, tie and felt hat climb out of the cockpit."

McCabe met Lindbergh again in 1944 on the small island of Green, near Rabaul. McCabe was able to talk with Lindbergh, and obtained Lindbergh's signature on a dollar bill which he covets among his memorabilia to this day.

McCabe flew 86 combat missions, mostly over Rabaul, finally leaving the military in 1946. He currently lives in Overland Park with his wife, Virginia, who is an expert in the restoration of rush and cane chairs. Their son, Ron, a Vietnam veteran, resides in Kansas City, Missouri.

McCabe's OS2U

McCabe as Navy cadet in 1942

Chapter 19

Leonard V. Porter, Jr.
Career Military Pilot

A "Missouri Boy"
Porter took his first breath in 1921 on a farm near the small town of Smithton, Missouri. He was the fourth in line of two brothers and two sisters. When he was two years old his family moved to the northeast section of Kansas City, Missouri.

In Kansas City, Porter worked in his father's ice house and, also learned the trade of being a "soda jerk" in a drug store. Not long after graduating from Northeast High School, Porter moved in with some friends in California until he found a job in a restaurant at the Van Nuys Airport.

The owner of the control tower provided Porter with a room in the tower, and flying lessons in a small Luscombe, if he would keep an eye on the un-manned control tower. During this time, Porter met some of the Hollywood stars who frequented the Van Nuys Airport to take advantage of air-travel.

In 1941 Porter returned to the Kansas City area. While working for Chrysler Motor Parts Company, he dated a young lady he had known in high school named Martha Kilcrease. The romantic sparks flew, and they were married before the year ended.

As 1942 began, Porter, now married and working at the B-25 plant in the Fairfax district of Kansas City, Kansas, felt that he was about to be snagged by his draft board.

He preferred to go into the military as an officer. Consequently, he reported to the Court House in Kansas City, Kansas to take an examination to enter the USAAF Flight Training Program. Porter was one of the three, out of 13 who took the test and passed.

Flight Training

On a cold morning in December 1942 a group of young men, excited and anxious about their future, gathered at the Union Station in Kansas City, Missouri to be transported to unfamiliar places throughout the United States. Newly married Porter was one of them. He said his good-bys to family members, and climbed aboard the train that would transport him to the Lackland Army Air Base outside of San Antonio, Texas.

Porter smiles as he remembers those first days at Lackland. Young men were issued shirts and shoes that didn't fit, and caps that fell down over their ears. It was the first time, for some of the recruits, that they had been cursed at.

Porter was classified as a pilot, and sent to preflight training which included more military discipline and harassment. He was referred to as a "maggot" by the upper classmen. Porter was subjected to classroom study and, and even though a poor student in high school, performed well.

After graduating from Preflight, Porter was assigned to Primary Flight Training in Muskogee, Oklahoma. His first flight in a PT-19 ended up with him "barfing". He "barfed" on his next five training flights and was on the pilot elimination list. But, on April Fool's Day, he made a flight without "barfing", and was able to remain in pilot training.

By the time Porter had graduated from Primary in April 1943, he had logged over 63 hours in the PT-19, learned to fly aerobatics proficiently (especially the "vertical reverse"), and was "top rated pilot" of his class. He was nicknamed "Chaplain" by his peers because he seemed adept at listening to his comrades' woes. He had also experienced the thrill of flying so low over a farmer's field, that the farmer jumped from his tractor while it was still running, and ran to his house. The farmer stood there shaking his fist in the air at Porter.

Porter left Oklahoma to attend Basic Flight School in Winfield, Kansas. At Winfield, Porter flew the BT-13 "Vultee Vibrator". At the end of Basic, Porter was awarded the honor of being first in the ground school classes, and number one rated in flying. According to Porter, "It made me wonder where I was (or my mind) in high school. After logging over 78 hours in the BT-13, Porter was sent to Pampa Army Air Field near Pampa, Texas. While there he learned to fly the Curtis AT-9 and the Cessna AT-17, both twin engines. Like most pilots, Porter didn't like the flying characteristics of the AT-9, even though he had become a "Cadet Instructor Pilot" for that particular airplane.

In October 1943 Porter graduated from Advanced Flight Training, and his wife, Marty, pinned his Wings on him. Shortly afterward, newly minted Second Lieutenant Porter received orders to report to Liberal, Kansas to learn to fly the famous B-24 Liberator bomber.

Combat Training

"Learning to fly the B-24 was dangerous, demanding and rigorous," writes Porter in his book, *Reflections of a Pilot, 1942 to 1964.* "...we rarely, if ever, were allowed to complete a takeoff without the simulated "loss" of at least one engine." Several men were killed from deadly B-24 crashes while at Liberal. The Liberator was a good airplane. But most pilots agreed that it took muscle strength sometimes to make it do what the pilot wanted it to do. After mastering the B-24, Porter picked up his assigned crew members, and traveled by train to Tonopah, Nevada where the whole crew would train together as a combat unit.

While at Tonopah, Porter and his crew came within a matter of seconds of losing their lives. On a night training flight near Phoenix, Arizona, Porter's aircraft suddenly was enveloped by a cloud which contained a great deal of turbulence. The instructor pilot, a captain, riding in the right seat ordered Porter to relinquish the controls. The B-24 entered a right spiral descent at 6,000 feet per minute descent rate. The captain continued to make corrections in the wrong directions. The B-24 was out of control. It was shaking so much from speed and turbulence that Porter could barely read the instruments.

Porter ordered his co-pilot to pull the captain from the controls. The B-24 was exceeding 400mph. It took every ounce of strength for Porter to haul the nose up. He was, however, able to stabilize the airplane just seconds before impacting the ground. For some unexplained reason, they had missed some mountains. The whole thing was scary and intense. The instructor pilot did not interfere. In fact, he said nothing. He was in a silent daze.

Once on the ground, Porter appeared before a group of officers in the Commander's office where he was asked to explain the incident. When finished explaining the near death situation, the Commander reprimanded Porter for the manner in which he talked to a Superior officer (the captain). But, the Commander finished his remarks by commending Porter for his quick actions in saving his crew and the airplane. They never saw the captain again. Porter learned a valuable lesson--one he never forgot. He decided that in future situations of that nature, he would take the controls sooner, and apologize to the superior later. According to Porter, "I began to implement this new modus operandi right away and improved on it during the rest of my career."

Flight to the Pacific

After combat training, Porter and his crew were told to report to Hamilton Field, California to be processed for overseas duty. After being processed, and receiving their combat pistols, knives and other small items, they flew to Fairfield-Suisun Army Air Field near San Francisco, California for deployment.

In June 1944 Porter's crew flew their new B-24J for a 13 hour and 40 minute trip from Fairfield-Suisun to Hickam Field on the island of Oahu in Hawaii. The crew felt very proud of themselves and their navigation. Out of 12 B-24s and eight B-25s that left California that day for Hawaii, only six B-24s and three B-25s made it to Hickam.

While at Hickam Field, eight B-24s were ordered to fly to Midway as a show of support, since only navy personnel had been there after the big battle. Of the eight B-24s in the flight, only Porter's airplane, which fought horrible weather, arrived at Midway. Porter couldn't praise his navigator, Joe Koivisto, enough.

In September 1944, after landing on Johnson Island to refuel, and Kwajalein Island for minor repairs, the crew landed their B-24J, *Ruff Knights,* on Saipan's single compacted 6800 feet landing strip.

Porter's crew settled in with the Seventh Air Force, 38th Bomb Squadron. The four officers lived in one tent, and the six enlisted crewmen in another. The mosquitoes were intense. Within a couple of weeks Porter contacted "Dengue" fever, also known as "Breakbone" fever and was very ill. He did not, however, ground himself.

Combat

At the time, the crews were required to fly 25 missions before they were rotated back to the United States. Porter's first combat mission entailed bombing an island north of Saipan called, Pagan. It was more of a practice run than anything, and not too heavily defended.

Porter's second combat mission was the first of several raids on Chichi Jima. Chichi Jima, part of the Bonin Island Group, is 150 miles north of Iwo Jima, and 600 miles from Japan. The island was the main communications center for Japan, and was extensively fortified. After being heavily bombed in 1943, the Japanese moved all but 25,000 troops off of the island.

Of the 22 American fliers shot down over Chichi Jima, eight were executed, and some were eaten. President George W. H. Bush, flying a TBM, was shot down in the area and was very fortunate to have evaded capture by the Japanese on shore that saw him go down.

It was a very scary place to be interned. After the war a trial was held on Guam, which brought to light many of the atrocities, and some of the Japanese military who committed them.

Mission to Chichi Jima

On their bombing raid on Chichi Jima's harbor, "Everybody was scared and pretty uptight," recalls Porter. They ran into the black bursts of anti-aircraft fire, and the hot burning phosphorous streamers which would fall on the airplane and burn. While on the bomb run Porter experienced a "run away" engine, and had to shut it down. After landing Porter observed holes in the tail of the B-24, which the crew voted to name *Ruff Knights*.

Porter's next three missions were to Chichi Jima, and on one of them he escorted a crippled B-24 back to Saipan, and both bombers ran out of fuel on the taxiway. His sixth mission was on a Sunday and his target was Iwo Jima. Porter faced his first enemy fighters on the run. Because the lead plane had to abort the mission, Porter's crew took the lead and achieved 100% hits in the target area. Porter was presented with the Distinguished Flying Cross for the mission.

Porter's crew flew bomb runs to Iwo Jima and Chichi Jima for the next six missions. They were accustomed to seeing enemy fighters, and on a raid Porter's gunners were listed with two "probable kills". By this time, several crew members in other squadron aircraft were injured by enemy fire and flak. The Japanese were dropping various types of bombs from above tied together with chains. The intent was for the bombs to snag on any part of the B-24s below and explode.

Ruff Knight destroys a Japanese cargo ship

On a bombing mission to Chichi Jima, the cloud cover over Chichi Jima made it difficult to see the target. On the way to Chichi Jima, Porter's crew had spotted three enemy ships in the harbor off an island called Haha Jima. Since they couldn't unload their six 500 pound bombs on Chichi Jima, they decided to make a run on the ships. Porter was at about 800 feet when he rounded a mountain on Haha Jima and spotted the three ships. *Ruff Knights* was going fast, and Porter pulled the power back to slow down, and headed for the center ship. The crew barely got the bomb bay doors open in time to drop their bombs. One of the bombs hit "dead center" on the middle ship, and according to Porter, "literally blew it to pieces." Shortly after the bombs had been released, number four engine failed, and the Liberator returned to Saipan on three engines. After returning to base the crew found the number of missions required before going home had been raised, again, (from the original 25 to 30) to 40.

Six days after sinking the ship in Haha Jima, Porter's crew received credit for another ship "possibly sunk". In November the squadron received their first fighter escorts in the form of the Lockeed P-38 Lightenings. According to Porter, "What a welcome sight! Our fighters made quick work of four "Zeke" Jap fighter aircraft that came up to attack us. Surprise! We had heavy, accurate flak though. Flying formation was very dangerous over the target due to poor flying by some of the pilots. We were lucky to hang in there and get good bomb hits. If it isn't one thing to scare the s_ _t out of you, it's another."

On December 7th United States time, 110 B-24s, plus B-29s and P-38s attacked Iwo Jima. Porter recalls that he, "couldn't see for all the flak" His B-24 was hit in three different places.

After his 19th mission, Porter was sent to Hawaii for almost a month of rest and recreation. Two days after he returned to Saipan, he flew to Iwo Jima on his 20th mission. On a mission to Truk the flak was very heavy. The P-38 escort shot four fighters down, and one P-38 was lost to flak.

Combat continues

In the meantime, the crew of a C-47 which regularly flew supplies and personnel between Saipan and Guam became ill. Porter, although never having flown a C-47, volunteered to fill in as pilot for a few days. When Porter reached the flight line, he told the crew chief that it had been some time since he had flown a C-47. He asked the crew chief to refresh him on the starting procedures, which he did. For the next two days Porter, his copilot and flight engineer flew three trips between Saipan and Guam; during which time they brought a supply of beer back to Saipan which they stole from the navy on Guam.

On another mission to Chichi Jima the weather was terrible with ice and snow. Porter's Liberator iced over. Even with full power, he almost stalled out at 150 mph. One B-24 was so flak damaged that he had to ditch in the sea. Porter descended to 500 feet looking for the crew. The downed crew was never heard from again.

Since the Japanese repaired the damage of the bombings at night, the B-24s began conducting bombing raids at night.

After his 35th mission, Porter's crew was moved to Guam and was integrated into the 11th Bomb Group, 42nd Bomb Squadron. He flew his last five missions from Guam to Chichi Jima. His 41st, and last mission, was flown just six months and one day from his first one.

During those six months, Porter was in the thick of combat. He faced severe flak on most occasions, along with enemy fighters. His *Ruff Knights* was hit many times, and his gunners were credited with many probables. He bombed airfields, ships and Mt. Suribachi. He was ready to go home.

Back to the States and Marty

Porter returned to the States in April 1945. Porter and his wife piled into their newly purchased 1941 maroon Buick sedan with the white sidewall tires and headed to Florida for a "rest and processing" period. He had accumulated enough "points" to qualify for military discharge. However, he and Marty decided that he would remain in the military.

Porter was ordered to Smyrna, Tennessee Army Air Field where he became a B-24 Instructor Pilot and Weather Briefing Officer. While there, he also flew T-6s and B-17s. He preferred flying the B-24 over the B-17.

Porter served at Lackland Air Base near San Antonio as a Supply Officer where he flew C-47s and B-25s. Later he was assigned to Ladd Air Base near Fairbanks, Alaska where he had some hair-raising flying experiences flying in the fridged weather and landing on snow and ice.

After a stint in Wichita, Porter was assigned to Randolph AFB, Texas to B-29 Bomber school, and later to MacDill AFB in Florida to the 305th Air Refueling Squadron to learn to fly the KC-97, a huge four engine airplane.

While at MacDill, flying at night, Porter had two experiences with unidentified flying objects. One incident was a very near miss by a cigar shaped object with lights, longer and larger than his KC-97. The other incident involved observing them at a distance flying parallel with him for awhile. Then suddenly, they would dart away at a very high speed. Both times, upon landing, he was met by authorities who told him to say nothing of the event.

In 1954 Captain Porter was assigned to the Strategic Air Command at Thule, Greenland. Porter left Greenland for McGuire AFB where he was given instruction in the C-118 (DC-6) Cargo aircraft, in which later he was classified as Senior Pilot.

He flew regular routes to Europe, (many of them to Germany) the Middle East and Greenland, and to Cuba during the Cuban crises. Porter's flights to countries all over the globe, and the people he met around the world, proved to be experiences he will always remember. After 22 years, Porter retired from the USAF in 1964 as a Lt. Colonel.

Aftermath

In 1964 Porter accepted a job with TWA as an Airline Captain. His job was in Jeddah, Saudi Arabia flying routes and providing instruction to Saudi Nationals. From that point, he, his wife Marty, and his son David, traveled the world. After spending 15 years with TWA, he retired in 1981.

The following is from an article in:

The Kansas City Star, February 19, 1945

"Plainsmen" do a job

Seventh Air Force Heavy Bomber Base in the Marianas, Feb 9—The "Atoll Busters" are causing the Japanese the loss of a lot of sleep, as well as more serious discomforts, in their unrelenting around the-clock bombing of the Bonin islands to pin down the Japanese air force.

Taking off from this island base, the huge 4-motored Liberators have been blasting Iwo Jima's only big Jap airstrip in the Bonin's. Day and night they have been pock-marking the field, burning planes and sinking ships within 650 miles of the Japanese homeland.

It is a continuous harassment. Today was the sixty-seventh consecutive day the Bombers had given Iwo Jima the around-the-clock treatment. Large flights strike in formation in the daytime, while single planes shuttle over the field at night about forty-five minutes apart, a practice not conducive to Japanese rest.

So successful has the bombing been that the Japanese have been unable to use Iwo Jima as a jumping off place for attacks on the Marianas, including the big B-29 nest at Saipan. That point has had no air raids in more than a month.

Typical of the youngsters softening the Bonins is Lieut. Leonard V Porter. Jr. 3604 Central Street, Kansas City, Missouri. Porter is a tall, blond of 23 years who has had twenty-eight missions.

"The flak is pretty heavy," he said "It comes up in bursts of black or white smoke and the phosphorus shells shoot out streamers. It naturally isn't fun when they are shooting at you. Sometimes at night they catch us in the searchlights and we have to take evasive action"

MAKES A SHIP "DISAPPEAR"

Last November Lieutenant Porter's crew put a bomb in the middle of a Japanese cargo ship at Haha Jima. The result, he said, was that, "one minute you saw a ship and the next there was nothing but splinters." "One of my biggest thrills," he continued. "was to have fighter cover. We've had it several times. Once over Iwo Jima a twin-engine Jap fighter was coming towards us. Three P-47's peeled off, one shot off his tail, the second hit his engine, and the third blew him up. Another time we had P-38's and it was a beautiful sight to see two of them hit a Jap fighter which burst into a ball of fire."

Lieutenant Porter is the son of Mr. and Mrs. Leonard V. Porter, 533 So. Hardesty Avenue. He is a former student of Northeast High School and later worked for the Chrysler Company in the Fairfax district. His wife, Mrs. Martha Porter, lives at 3604 Central Street.

Cadet Porter   **Lt. Colonel Leonard V. Porter**

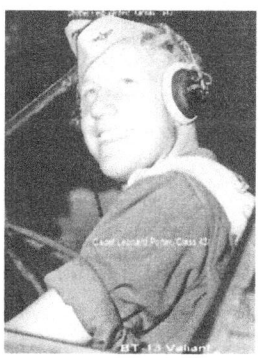 

Porter delivering supplies to Ellsmere Island, Greenland in a C-47.

BELOW: Other aircraft Porter flew. B29 & KC-97

FACE WEST

I hope there's a place, way up in the sky
Where pilots can go when they have to die.
A place where a guy can buy a cold beer
For a friend and a comrade whose memory is dear.
A place where no doctor or lawyer could tread,
Nor a management type would e'er be caught dead.

Just a quaint little place, kind of dark, full of smoke,
Where they like to sing loud and tell a good joke.
The kind of a place where a lady could go
And feel safe and protected by the men they would know.
There must be a place where old pilots go
When their wings get too weary and their airspeed gets slow.

Where the whiskey is old and the women are young,
And the songs about flying and dying are sung.
Where you'd see all the fellows who had gone west before
And they'd call out your name as you came through the door.
Who would buy you a drink if your thirst should be bad
And relate to the others "He was quite a good lad!"

And then through the mist you would spot an old guy
You had not seen in years, though he'd taught you to fly.
He's nod his old head and grin ear to ear,
And say, "Welcome, my son, I am glad you are here.
For this is the place true fliers come
When the battles are over and the wars have been won.

"They've come here at last to be safe and as far
From the government clerk and the management czar,
Politicians, lawyers, the feds, and the noise…
Where all the hours are happy and these good old boys
Can relax with a cool one and a well deserved rest,
This is heaven, my son. You have passed your last test."

-Capt. Michael Larkin, TWA

BOOK VI

Vietnam

Chapter 20

Peter Illman
Combat Marine

Background

It was in the early 1960s when young Paul Edward Illman's (commonly referred to as *Pete,* or *Hooter)* life merged with mine. I had been out of the United States Navy for about six years, and out of college for only about two or three years. My first job was teaching eighth graders at what was then known as Indian Hills Junior High School at 63rd and Mission Road. I taught an educational concept called unified studies; (I called it untied studies) which was a two or three hour block of time, and included history, English and some science. Like most new educational *breakthroughs,* that concept is now history too, and should be.

One day the principal called me into his office and announced that he had rounded up a group of students who, let us say, *marched to a different drum beat* than the beat of the traditionally accepted one of the school. Many of these students did not have much respect for the authoritarian policies laid down by the teachers and the administrators. The principal told me that he had enough of these students to fill a unified studies class; and, according to him, I was going to be the teacher. Because I had been teaching some accelerated classes, I didn't have a feeling of joy when I received my new assignment. The class consisted mostly of boys. When I met the class for the first time; that's where I met 13 year old Pete Illman.

Show and tell

Pete was born, and grew up in the greater Kansas City metropolitan area. He attended grade school and junior high in the Shawnee Mission School District   Pete's opening remarks during the interview for this piece were, "I remember when I met you. It was in that kind of *special* class; A class of *crazies.*" It was during this class that Pete and his buddy, Frank Baum, asked me if they could *milk* a poisonous snake in my classroom. Being young and foolish, I granted them their wish ... The three of us engaged in a serious conversation about their expertise with snakes, and the safety of the classroom.

Sure enough, on the assigned day, Pete and Frank arrived in the classroom with a long pole with a wire hoop on the end of it, a glass jar and a glass cage with a live copperhead inside. It occurred to me then, that I may have made a huge mistake. But I wasn't going to renege on my promise. I ordered all of the students to vacate their desks and stand by the rear wall of the classroom. What I witnessed next was amazing.

Pete and Frank opened the cage; Pete held the snake just behind its head and began massaging it as it spit the poison venom into a glass jar. Within a few minutes they placed the snake back into its cage, and removed it from the classroom. The event was over. Thank God!

These two thirteen year old boys approached their task as serious professionals. They were experienced snake hunters, and I understand, remained so for most of their lives ... Needless to say, Pete and Frank were now heroes in the eyes of the other students in the class. Pete has since told me that some of the educators looked critically upon our event. However, neither administrator nor teacher ever voiced that concern to me personally.

It is imperative that I relate to you that I have always remembered that class more than any of the others. 1 grew to really enjoy that class; they were really good kids, and we got along well with each other. It is interesting to note that the students in this *special* class performed every bit as well as the students in my accelerated class.

Vietnam

After completing the eighth grade, Pete attended Saint John's Military Academy in Salina, Kansas where he attained the rank of battalion commander before he graduated in 1967.

After Saint John's, "I attended Kansas University for a semester," recalls Pete. "But I didn't like that because I already knew how to drink beer and chase women." Pete considered himself destined for something else. Thus in 1968 Pete traveled to Emporia, Kansas and enlisted in the United States Marine Corps.

Because of the war, boot camp in San Diego, California was reduced from 16 weeks to 10 weeks. "It was tough," remembers Pete. Because of his academy training, Pete was one of the few that were given the rate of PFC after boot camp.

Pete was assigned to Camp Pendleton, California for infantry and weapons training. After going home on leave, he returned to the staging area at Camp Pendleton where he was shipped out to Viet Nam.

Pete was designated as an anti-tank assault man. He had trained on the 106 mm recoilless rifle, the 3.45 inch bazooka, the flame-thrower, the LAW anti tank weapon and demolitions. According to Pete, "The flame-thrower weighed 70 pounds. It was heavy and dangerous. You had to make sure it was aimed at what you wanted to hit before setting it off. Also, you had to make damned sure you fired it downwind. We never used them. We filled them with water and had squirt gun fights."

During combat helicopter landings, several waves of choppers, each carrying about 16 men, dropping down and landing. As soon as the chopper landed, the men would jump out and establish a perimeter. With each future landing the perimeter would be expanded. "At first light," remembers Pete, "we would move out. And the place was just filled with booby traps."

During one patrol a good buddy of Pete's (a marine who had just extended his tour) was point man for the platoon. As he walked under some overhead foliage he was killed by an explosive that was detonated by a Viet Cong (VC) soldier. When others of the platoon rushed to drag him out, more marines were killed. According to

Pete, "When it was all over, we were down to one squad left. We did manage to shoot the VC out of the tree with a machine gun."

Most of the time when Pete's unit went out to *Indian country,* they were out for 28 days, and returned to camp for two days. While in the field Pete ate two meals of C rations a day. They carried some rations with them, and were supplied with C rations dropped by helicopters. "That wasn't a bad thing," said Pete, "except when the weather socked us in and the choppers couldn't get to us. One time we went three days without food. Also, without the helicopter drops, we ran low on ammunition."

Every night at about dusk, Pete's unit would pretend to dig-in in a circular perimeter. "After dark," recalls Pete, "we would all move about 300 yards, because we knew the VC were watching us. When the VC didn't know exactly where we were, they had to probe our lines; and that's when we were able to get a lot of kills.

At night, along with our starlight scopes, we used our ears and our nose all of the time, because your eyes could deceive you. We utilized the pilot's scan. You moved your eyes around, and if you were going to see something, you would see it in a split second."

The stench of the VC was penetrating. The VC lived in caves, but the marines could usually smell them. "They smelled like fish and urine. Sometimes when they smoked dope outside our lines, we could really smell it. They would get all hopped-up, (most likely on opium) and we knew they were going to attack."

In fact, Pete's unit was lucky to get a bath during their *in-country* patrols, and when they did it was usually in a stream or a river. In a river, the marines would take off their clothes and scrub themselves down with sand from the river bottom. The marines never used shaving lotion or soap because the VC would smell them. They would not shave or cut their hair for four weeks at a time. "The beard and longer hair helped to facilitate their camouflage. They never smoked during the night.

Most of the fighting was at night. If the VC probed and found a hole in the lines, they could pretty much determine the location of the rest of the perimeter. On at least one of Pete's patrols they fought every night for 28 consecutive nights. "They say the VC owned the night," recalls Pete. "But that was not true. We had better weapons; we owned the night."

The war for Pete was a love/hate thing. "I hated being there," said Pete. "But in a fire-fight, if we had the jump on them, it was fun." Pete's most interesting job was going out with the scouts in a six man team. "We carried an M-14, no flak jackets, and no helmets," said Pete. "We traveled light. We could go anywhere we wanted and do what ever we wanted. We were working with S-2, intelligence, and were really under no one's control. We moved quickly, and killed anything that got in the way."

A lot of the fighting *in-country* was over food, especially rice and com. There was a large rice-growing triangle south of Da Nang, located near the old industrial city of An Hoa, which was about 15 miles inland, and near the foot of the mountains. But most of the fields had been destroyed. The small villages could grow only enough rice for themselves. In order to keep the VC from raiding and destroying the villages for food, the American units attempted to destroy the villages first. According to Pete, "All of the wild animals had been hunted down and slaughtered for food." Deer and wild boor, which at one time had been common to the area, were never seen.

Many of the enemy were seasoned veterans who had fought the Japanese, the French and the Americans. And, according to Pete, "...were damned good." We were within pistol range of the VC and the North Vietnamese Army," recalls Pete, "basically all the time I was there." Everywhere we went there were mine fields. There were Viet Cong, South Vietnamese, North Vietnamese, Japanese, French and American mine fields; and the Americans were the only ones that ever mapped-out where they placed the mines."

The marines didn't know at the time, nor did our government, that the water they bathed in, the water they drank, and the water which they doggedly trudged through was tainted with Agent Orange. Pete is drawing 100 percent disability at this time, and 90 percent of it was awarded due to the effects of his constant exposure to Agent Orange.

The environment of constantly being in the vicinity of the enemy made Pete nervous at first. "But after awhile," said Pete, "you get used to it and you know that you are going to live, or die." It was always comforting for Pete to know that the man next to him was a well-trained marine. One night, every man in Pete's unit was totally exhausted, and soaked through to the skin from rain. "It was very rare when a marine fell asleep when on watch," said Pete. But as NCO in charge that night, I spent my time going through the ranks kicking the men in their heads to keep them awake."

"Our unit didn't get many medals," recalls Pete. "But we were not out there for medals. We were out there for ourselves." Some of the officers and men who stayed behind, and did receive awards, were referred to in derogatory terms as *Remington Raiders;* which meant they stayed behind and typed forms and letters on their Remington typewriters.

There were some laughable moments for Pete during his combat tour. He remembers visiting Da Nang with some of his combat buddies and stealing jeeps and driving them back to his camp. When his Capitan saw them coming, he immediately hustled the jeeps to an area when they could be repainted. "Hell," recalls Pete, "I think we had half of the jeeps in Da Nang." This was the same company commander who had risen through the enlisted ranks to become a captain. According to Pete, sometimes the captain would get drunk in the *club,* and on the way back to his quarters he would run into the razor-sharp barbed wire surrounding the helicopter pad, and become entangled. "Then," remembers Pete, "He would yell, 'Come and get me you bastards.' So we ran out, pulled him out, bandaged him-up, and threw him into the sack." Pete remembers that sometimes during the heat of a fight, some marine would say, "Hell, this is just like a WWII movie without the music."

Pete spent 13 months on his tour in Viet Nam, before he was slated to return to the United States. When he told his CO that he wanted to extend for another tour, the CO told Pete, "No, you are beginning to like this too much." Pete returned home and decided that college was not for him.

Pete had an interest in flying, and had been flying since he was 13 years old in his father's Cherokee private airplane. Since Pete held the multi-engine, commercial and instrument ratings, he flew cable patrol in Kansas, Nebraska, Iowa and Wyoming for AT&T. These pilots flew many hours, and at an altitude of 100 feet. After a couple of years Pete sold his contract to another person. This person flew the patrol alone instead of two people as Pete did. On his second flight he crashed and killed himself.

Later Pete flew left seat with an instructor as a mail courier in Aero Commanders for John Towner (another ex student of mine at Shawnee Mission East). Pete worked for an air freight company in Kansas City for about ten years and finally gave up flying because of diabetes. Because of his physical problems, he has never been able to pass a flight exam

The war took its toll on Pete. He still has good days, and bad days. When he is not in Kansas City, he is visiting friends in Mexico, Georgia, Alabama or various other locations where he can get a little R&R and fellowship. He keeps in touch with some of his Vietnam buddies.

Pete is very knowledgeable about aviation and military history. Pete may be a tough old marine, but his heart is as large as the inside of a USAF C-5, which is one of the world's largest cargo aircraft. Who would ever have guessed that the scrawny 13 year old boy, who was one of my students, would end up being one of my heroes.

BELOW: Marine Sgt. Pete (Hooter) Ill in Viet Nam fixing himself some coffee.

BELOW: A photograph Pete took of the Marine just in front of him.

Chapter 21

Kathy (Sullivan) Lee
Army Nurse

Kathy Lee was born as Kathy Sullivan on a cold day in December 1946 in Sommerville, Massachusetts. When Sullivan was nine months old her mother died. Before Sullivan was even born, however, her father had gone to the store to purchase a loaf of bread, and never returned. Sullivan first saw her father when she was twenty one years old. After the death of her mother, Sullivan was sent to Welfleet, on the Cape, to live with her grandfather.

After five years Sullivan and her two sisters went to live with her aunt who lived with a couple called Myrtle and Pop, in a boarding house in Plymouth, Massachusetts. Myrtle and Pop (Pop was from the "old country") were in their sixties. Pop owned cranberry bogs, and Sullivan helped him harvest the cranberries with a wooden scoop. "Pop was one of the greatest men I ever knew," recalls Sullivan. Pop lived to be 101 years old, and at 82 he gave Sullivan away at her wedding. To this day she still misses the sounds of the seagulls and the smell of the ocean.

Nursing school

Sullivan attended grades one through twelve in Plymouth. Sullivan's aunt, who was a nurse, dictated from early age that Sullivan would also become a nurse. Her aunt told her that since they were living on state funds, there would be no money for education. Sullivan would have to find a way to fund her education. Sullivan worked very hard in high school and after graduation, with the help of three scholarships; she enrolled in nurses training at Quincy City Hospital in Quincy, Massachusetts. Her scholarships provided enough money to get her through the first two years of training. When she reached her third year of training, she was out of money.

Sullivan had reached the proverbial *fork in the road*. She felt that she would have to drop out of nurse's training and go to work. She was afraid, however, that if she did, she might not return to school.

While in school, army recruiters visited the campus in an attempt to entice students to join the army, and have their third year of nursing paid for by Uncle Sam. It was the fork in the road that Sullivan chose. Sullivan enlisted in the Army Nurse Corps. Sullivan had to commit to three years of service, but upon graduation she would receive her nursing diploma, and a commission as a second lieutenant.

After *passing the boards,* Sullivan was commissioned a 2nd Lieutenant and ordered to Fort Sam Houston, Texas for six weeks of basic training. In March of 1968 Sullivan was assigned to Walter Reed Army Hospital in Washington, D.C. where she learned to love pediatrics. She thought highly of her chief nurse, who retired from the U.S. Army as a lieutenant colonel, and to whom she still corresponds with today. While at Walter Reed Sullivan began to hear stories and talk about Vietnam. She had always had thoughts about the Peace Corps; and she thought that maybe Vietnam was a place where she could do some good. "I didn't know anything about war," recalls Sullivan. "I was only 21 years old. But I thought I would give it a try; I wanted to help our soldiers." Sullivan volunteered for duty in Vietnam. After returning home on a 30 day leave, she shipped out to war on December 26, 1968.

Vietnam

Twenty one year old Sullivan took off from Boston during a severe snow storm. She arrived by air at Bien Hoa, in southern Vietnam, on December 31, 1968. The temperature was a sweltering 126 degrees. She was assigned to the 90th Replacement Center. After landing, there was a great deal of noise. Sullivan assumed that the soldiers were having a great time celebrating New Years Eve. She soon learned, however, that an attack was in process and the noise was from bombs, rockets and guns. That was not the only time that Sullivan's naïveté would be punctured.

Sullivan had been exposed to some army training which explained the weather, booby traps and punji sticks. But according to Sullivan, "All of that stuff didn't apply to me; I was going to be a nurse in a hospital." She had even brought her white shoes to the war zone because she thought that she was going to work in a hospital where the nurses wore white.

When Sullivan reported to the supply department, the sergeant asked her what size shoes she wore. Sullivan replied, "I wear size 5. I brought my own white shoes. Why do you want to know?" The sergeant handed her a pair of combat boots, six pairs of combat fatigues, a flack jacket and a helmet. Sullivan told the sergeant that he was wrong. Sullivan pushed the clothing back to him saying, "You don't understand, I'm a nurse, I wear all white." The sergeant pushed the clothing back to her with the comment, "Not this year, Ma'am." Sullivan began to think that something was not quite right. This was not at all what she had expected.

Five days later, Sullivan was ordered to pack up and board a C-130, which deposited her at Chu Lai, Vietnam during a heavy monsoon downpour. Chu Lai was located right on the South China Sea, and by helicopter, about 30 minutes south of Da Nang. She was assigned to the 312th Evac. Hospital. The hospital consisted of individual Quonset Huts with the typical corrugated aluminum roofs. When it rained the noise was unbearable. Without air conditioning, the huts became insufferable. Each unit held 50 beds. Sullivan was assigned two enlisted corpsmen to assist her in the ward. She worked 12 and 13 hours a day, seven days a week.

Sullivan was not impressed by her duty station. "I just did not like it," recalls Sullivan. After about a month at Chu Lai, she went to her commander and explained to him that she didn't like it here. "I told the colonel," recalls Sullivan, "that this is not what I expected. I had volunteered to come here; and now I was volunteering to go back."

The C.O. asked Sullivan how long she had been in-country. When he learned that she had been there for only a month, he told her that he couldn't do that. The colonel stated that it would be eleven months before he could sign the papers to rotate her back to the states.

Sullivan replied, "Colonel, I'm not kidding or being funny. How long will it take you to sign the papers for me to leave?" The C.O. replied, "Lieutenant, you need to understand that you are not going anywhere; I will be leaving before you do." Sullivan finally got the point. It would be eleven and a half more months before Sullivan flew out of Vietnam. A few months later when the colonel's time was up, he dropped by to see Sullivan while she was on duty. He said to her, "Goodbye, I'm going home and you're not."

Casualties of war

The ugly reality of the horrible war which was being fought in Vietnam presented itself to Sullivan immediately when she was assigned to the Triage and the recovery rooms. It was difficult for her to assimilate what she was witnessing. Handling Triage was very difficult and heart rendering. Even today, Sullivan remembers some of the decisions she had to make concerning the priority of medical care; and she hopes that she made the appropriate decisions, because some of the soldiers died before they were placed on the surgeons' tables.

Sullivan saw almost every kind of wound or injury known to mankind. She saw soldiers, flown in from combat landing zones in Huey Helicopters, with only pieces of their bodies. She helped unload one Huey that landed at the hospital with 11 wounded soldiers plus the helicopter crew. "I swear," recalls Sullivan, "I don't know how that helicopter even flew with all that weight. When we unloaded the Huey, we found that a few of the soldiers were already dead."

According to Sullivan, "My goals were to help them with the will to live; and to ensure that they received the best of care." Some of the first questions asked by the wounded were, "Did so-and-so (their buddy or friend) come in, too? Did so-and-so make it?" Sullivan was with a wounded soldier one time when he opened his eyes, then looked at her, and said, "Man, it's good to see round eyes again." Sometimes soldiers died while in the nurses' arms. Many times the nurses were the last people the wounded saw. On the way to the operating tables, soldiers would ask the nurses to write to their mothers and tell her that they loved her. It was common, of course, to see blood on a nurse's uniform, as well as the floor.

Vietnamese Ward

In April Sullivan was assigned to the Vietnamese Ward of the hospital. The ward was filled with young and old Vietnamese civilians, and Viet Cong Prisoners of War.

She was really not happy about administering medical aid to the Vietnamese. She felt that she had come to Vietnam to provide aid to

American soldiers—not to provide care for their enemies. None of the Vietnamese spoke English. That fact, plus the unfamiliar cultural divide, was very frustrating to her. Sullivan tried not to hold resentment toward the Vietnamese. Many of the Vietnamese civilian patients' families camped in the hospital ward with them. It was not an unusual scene to see ten or fifteen Vietnamese family members sleeping on the floor, under the bed, or on the bed with the patient.

At one point, Sullivan had a Vietnamese patient who kept pulling out the feeding tubes which were attached to him. As fast as Sullivan put them back in, he would pull them out. He was an *all around* problematic patient. Knowing he couldn't understand English, she uttered a few swear words at him. Suddenly, she heard someone say in English, that she shouldn't talk to him that way. She discovered that the words came from a Vietnamese patient in the bed next to her patient. It was the only Vietnamese that she had ever heard speak English. Sullivan scolded the person because he could have been a great deal of assistance as a translator in helping the patients and the nurses. He informed Sullivan that it was not his job, and that he was not going to become involved.

One of Sullivan's patients was an old Vietnamese man who had tuberculosis. He had difficulty keeping food off of his beard. The beard consisted of about six chin whiskers that were very, very long, and the food would cake-up and become crusty. In an attempt to solve the problem, Sullivan finally shaved the beard off one day when the old man was asleep. Some of the Vietnamese civilian patients saw what Sullivan had done, and jumped out of their beds and came after her. Several other Vietnamese non-patient civilians were furious and joined the attack. They were after Sullivan's hide. Sullivan had to run completely out of the ward for safety. She was later informed that the unsightly whiskers were sacred to the old man's religious beliefs; and that she had violated his religious convictions. The old man was lifted out immediately by helicopters to another hospital. Sullivan was immediately reassigned to the malaria ward because of "cultural reasons." Her replacement was a new nurse, First Lieutenant Sharon Lane.

Survivor's guilt

Sullivan had become friends with Lane during the six months that Lane had been assigned as a nurse at Chu Lai. Lane told

Sullivan, "I was assigned to the Vietnamese ward today." Sullivan replied, "Well, don't shave anyone." The next day Sullivan was working at her new assignment in the malaria ward which was only a hundred feet from the Vietnamese ward when she felt the ground shake, and heard a tremendously loud noise. The patients and the hospital staff dived to the floor. People were screaming and running in different directions. Donning her flack jacket, Sullivan ran outside of her ward and saw that the Vietnamese ward had been completely leveled to the ground. Twenty five year old Lt. Sharon Lane had been killed in the blast, the day after she had replaced Sullivan in the ward.

The staff was devastated over Lane's death. Sullivan felt all the emotions of fear, frustration and anger. She felt responsible for Lane being in the wrong place at the wrong time. She felt that it should have been her. This feeling is referred to as survivor's guilt; and Sullivan still has not shed some of those feelings to this day.

Not exactly a soldier

Twenty one year old, 100 pound, red-haired Sullivan did not always adhere strictly to military regulations. In one instance the soldiers in her ward were enjoying watching Bob Hope entertain some American troops on television. Since it was a little after "lights-out", a nurse of superior rank stopped by her ward and ordered the television turned off. Sullivan argued with her. But the superior turned it off anyway. After the superior left the ward, Sullivan turned it on again. The superior returned and was told by the patients that they had turned it back on. The superior, however, reported Sullivan, and she had to appear before the commanding officer. It was not pleasant. On a few occasions, against military regulations, she flew with a helicopter crew to a landing zone to bring back the wounded.

Sullivan has great admiration for the helicopter pilots for their bravery and commitment to rescuing and returning wounded soldiers. She even dated a few of the pilots on her off-time. Sullivan spoke highly of the doctors who unselfishly worked long hours, and used their skills to save the lives of the soldiers.

In December of 1969 Sullivan's Vietnam tour was near its completion. She was able to take advantage of a special program called Operation Santa Claus, to leave two weeks earlier. She jumped at the chance. When some of her cohorts suggested that she stay the last few weeks to see Bob Hope, who was scheduled to perform a Christmas show on the base, she declined. "I'll watch it on TV," exclaimed Sullivan.

Before leaving, she had to take her "exit interview" with the commanding officer. The C.O. told Sullivan (whose three year enlistment was about to end) that it was his job to speak with each departing nurse who was on verge of discharge to entice them into staying in the army. But to Sullivan, he suggested that maybe the US Army wasn't for her; she didn't seem to fit. Sullivan relayed to the C.O. that she whole heartedly agreed with every word he said, and replied, "When can I leave?" Kathy Sullivan left Vietnam for the United States on December 15, 1969, and was shocked by the reception she received upon arriving in San Francisco. During the following month, Sullivan accepted her honorable discharge from the United States Army.

Civilian nurse

Sullivan was confused by the hatred of some Americans toward the military when she returned. She was booed, and eggs and tomatoes were thrown at her. She became distressed by the questions she was asked. She learned not to tell people she had been in Vietnam. When people asked her where she was from, she replied, "The East coast." Well, Chu Lai was on the east coast of Vietnam.

Unwelcomed psychological scars are left on Sullivan today. For instance, she will not enter a Vietnamese restaurant because the smell of the food brings back memories of sickness, unhealthiness, dying and war.

After returning to the United States Sullivan served as a nurse in hospitals in Texas, Virginia, Chicago, and then in 1972 returned to Virginia where she worked in several hospitals, and married Don Lee, a man whom she had met before going to Vietnam. The Lees then moved to Springfield, Missouri where she worked at the Mount Vernon Hospital. The Lees moved back to Virginia where they sired two children, Andy and Ryan. In 1990 the Lees moved to the Blue Springs area, and finally settled in Oak Grove, Missouri. Because of her exposure to Agent Orange, Lee (now her married name) suffers from diabetes. She gave up nursing but went to work at the Veterans Hospital in Kansas City, Missouri.

Lee is a Veterans Service Officer for the Department of Missouri. She is passionately dedicated to helping American veterans. She has helped hundreds of former servicemen obtain services they needed; and for many, who didn't realize the benefits to which they were entitled. There is always a line at her office door.

A part of the past revisited

Lee could never erase the memory of Vietnam nurse Sharon Lane's death. She had often thought of contacting Lane's parents— but was reluctant because she was never sure if it was the right thing to do. Finally, in 1980, Lee obtained Lane's address, and composed a letter. She kept the letter for several months before she decided to send it. In the letter, Lee talked of how she knew Lane and how sorry she was over her death. Lee also told the parents that she understood if they didn't want to reply.

Lane's father had passed away in 1979; but Lane's mother and Lee corresponded for many years. A local Kansas City man named Chuck Wright who was a member of the Medical War Memorial, and co-author of *DOC, Medics, and Surgeons in Combat* paved the way for a meeting between Mrs. Lane and Lee.

The meeting took place at the Akron/Canton Ohio Airport in October 2005. Lee was met by Mrs. Lane and a group of the Sharon Lane Memorial Chapter 199 of the Vietnam Veterans of America (VVA) of Canton. It was a wonderful visit for Lee. When she first stood in front of Mrs. Lane, she said, "I'm sorry." Mrs. Lane replied, "Why? You have nothing to be sorry for." Those words brought peace to Lee's mind, and maybe, even some closure.

An active patriot

Lee is active in many veteran oriented organizations, and has held offices in most. She lists the VFW, VVA, Vietnam Veterans Association), MOA (Military Officers Association), CAF (Commemorative Air Force, Heart of America Wing), and the American Business Women's Association as some of the organizations to which she belongs.

Lee believes that all veterans, whether they sat at a desk, or faced the horrors of combat deserve to be honored and rewarded by our government.

Vietnam taught Lee to appreciate every day, and to respect her fellow man. She loves sunsets (some of the most beautiful in

Vietnam) because it means one has lived another full day. Kathy (Sullivan) Lee understands what America is, and what it should be. A plaque in her office reads:

>*America: We are many, yet we are one.*
>*We are different, and the same.*
>*We are a land of all colors, races and faiths. Above all, we are free*
>*That is what makes us America.*

Kathy at work in Chu Lai

Kathy in her bunker

Graduation at Ft Sam Houston.

"Bad –hair day" in Chu Lai

The Girl Next door (Combat Nurse)

She grew up in America, just the girl next door
Never thought to question what we were fighting for
They sent her off to war and showed her death and pain
And the girl next door will never be the same.

    Guarding her patients with a .45
    Checking the wounded to make sure they're alive
    By days she's in fatigues and at night she's in a dress
    She's everybody's savior, the Army combat nurse.

She told her girl friends "I'll see ya some old day
I've joined the army and they're sending me away."
They taught her how to mend a wound and how to tend the sick
But nothing could prepare her for all this.

    Guarding her patients with a .45
    Checking the wounded to make sure they're alive
    By days she's in fatigues and at night she's in a dress
    She's everybody's savior, the Army combat nurse.

Bridge:
Women at home waiting all alone
Women in life trying to do what's right
Women in war in the blood and gore
Women in death, they die just like the rest.

A jungle ain't a place for a girl to be alone
Surrounded by the enemy with all the soldiers gone
Under attack you know she's got to do her best
Because she's everybody's savior, the Army combat nurse.

Back home in civilian life army life all done
Childhood friends can't understand why she's not any fun
But a vision of the wounded screams inside her brain
And the girl next door will never be the same.

    Guarding her patients with a .45
    Checking the wounded to make sure they're alive
    By days she's in fatigues and at night she's in a dress
    She's everybody's savior, the Army combat nurse
    She's everybody's savior *(but her own)*, the Army combat nurse

...but who will save HER now?

BOOK VII

Letters Home

Chapter 22

Lloyd M. Langdon
KAI

Progression of the confidence of a young fighter pilot shown through his letters home.

C. J. Langdon, the sister of Lloyd Langdon, and the youngest of nine children, self-published a book containing all of the letters Langdon wrote home to his mother and father during the war years 1940-1944. In her book, *A Legacy of Letters*, C. J. Langdon wrote:

> Mom saved Lloyd's letters because it was all she and dad had left of a son who died at only 23 years of age. They were in a box in the attic, whether she ever went up there to reread them over the years, we'll never know. The folks never fully recovered from the loss of their young son in the war. Lloyd's picture was in a prominent place on the mantle over the fireplace until we sold the folk's house and packed all the memories it held away.
>
> After the folks were gone, the letters were kept in my house. When rereading them in 2002, it was apparent to me they were a reflection of life during those times and, for our family, a personal tragedy of that war. It seemed prudent that Lloyd's letters and this piece of history should be shared not only with my family, but anyone who has an interest in the events of that time.

Lloyd Langdon was the fourth born into a family of nine children. The Langdon family lived in a small suburban Kansas town near Kansas City, Missouri. Langdon wanted to be a pilot. When he applied to the US Army Air Corps, the recruiter told him that he would be better off in the regular ground units until he was fattened up some, and then transfer to the Air Corps later, which he did. He was assigned to the US Army's Cavalry Unit at Fort Riley, Kansas. I have chosen only four of the letters in C. J. Langdon's collection, because I believe that they give a "bird's eye" view of Lloyd Langdon's progression from a naïve recruit to an efficient combatant. The following letter was one of his first to his home:

Fort Riley, Kansas· October 30, 1941

Dear Mother

Received your letter yesterday. I was glad to get it. It was the first I received since I've been here.

Well I got two more shots yesterday and were they tough. Typhoid. They carried 6 men out of our barracks to the hospital last night. They took my temperature. It was 101.2. Didn't rate hospitalization. Stayed in bed all day though. Couldn't eat but half of one meal all day. Breakfast. Didn't eat until noon today. Feel somewhat better today though.

Just performed a good act, however. It turned out very funny. We have 1 or 2 fellows who can't write any more than their name. They're Indians from Texas. I wrote a letter for one. He thanked me and

went down to the mailbox with it. He had no stamps or money. But he wasn't so dumb. No! He just waited till no one was looking and threw in the letter without a stamp. I thought I'd die when he came back and told me how slick he was.

I have another funny thing to say but I'll put it in Pop's letter.

Love, your son, Lloyd.

Langdon applied for a transfer to the Air Corps, and after passing his examinations was assigned San Antonio, Texas.

San Antonio, Texas· November 14, 1942

Dear Dad:

I'm writing this letter because I know how interested you are in my training. I hope this will give you an idea of what it's like here.
To begin with, the discipline is more strict than you can ever imagine. We have to learn in 9 weeks what they learn in 9 months at West Point. Everything we do from reveille to taps is done under the uncompromising looks of upper classmen. We have to do some of the most absurd things I ever heard of and anyone caught laughing has to do something even sillier. I'm sitting here now (lucky me) and almost choking listening to what's going on in the aisle.

Almost everyone is drilling off smiles. A man on my left has 19 smiles and they are making him tuck each one in bed and sing it to sleep. I can hardly write I'm shaking so. We are subject to every known insult. Don't get me wrong, it's to teach us self-control and it really does the job.

The academic side of my training is just 3 hours a day now. It'll be later. I take Morse Code, math, and Army Organization, an hour each a day. We have to learn fast. I'll write more about it as we go along.

We started physical training in a big way today. That, like everything else, is pretty rough. We have a 3 mile cross country course and we have to run it in less than 22 minutes. You feel like your lungs are going to blow up.

We have a 2 hour study period each evening and an hour before bedtime to ourselves each night. That is, if we can keep from smiling.

I'll write again, Pop. Your son, Lloyd

In 1943 Langdon was transferred to Texas for primary flight training.

Bonham, Texas – January 28, 1943
Dear Dad:
I know that your birthday comes soon if it hasn't

already passed, so I thought I should at least take some time and tell you about my training. I know you are very much interested in how I'm doing. Here goes.

The trainers we have here are the very latest in design. They have flaps and all the other gadgets. They aren't small ships by any means. They have 185 horsepower and burn about 12 gallons of gas per hour. Almost any maneuver can be executed in one of them. They have a reputation for being a little tricky to learn on but when you do, you've got something. Our instructors say that the 60 hours we get here on these ships is worth 200 hours of C.P.T. I know they can sure make work out of flying, though.

My instructor is a typical Texan, easy going, but he's pretty bright. He owns a ranch somewhere and is always complaining because he can't get in as an Army pilot. He's about 35, I guess. He really knows his stuff. Today, I had a pretty good day. He told me to take off, climb to 3000 ft. and execute 2 normal recovery stalls and then a spin to the left. That sounds easy, but it involves quite a bit of thinking and maneuvering. Anyway, I did them all pretty good so he asked me if I had ever flown upside down. I said I had not and he told me to tighten my belt (safety belt). The damn thing was pretty loose and it wouldn't tighten but as I can't talk back (one way speaking system), he didn't know it. First, he did a few snap rolls and slow rolls. Then he put her into a

dive until we were doing about 180 and flipped her over on her back. He had to cut the motor as these engines can't be operated very long while upside down. He has a little mirror on his windshield so he can see back and give me h- for everything from not looking around to looking around too much. Anyway, I looked into the mirror and saw him looking at me and laughing. He asked me why I was hanging on so I put my arms out of the pit and just hung. The belt was so loose I
had about four inches between me and the seat. What a funny feeling to look up at the ground 4000 ft. below. It's lights out so I'll finish in the morning.

It's now Friday and I've just finished my hop for today. We started vertical banks today. I did about 8 and they were fair so I made 3 take offs and landings. That's what we have to do when we solo. We take off, fly the traffic pattern and then land. You have to do that three times and then you've soloed. My second landing was a six pointer. I hit three times on the wheels before I got the tail down. I've also made what my instructor calls Chinese takeoffs, one wing too low. But so far I'm one of a few fellows who haven't ground looped yet. These ships do that at the slightest excuse.

Well, I have about another hour before I can solo yet. We can't solo before 8 hours. We have until 17 hours. The washing machine goes to work next week so I'm afraid some of the boys will be leaving.

Actually some of them couldn't fly a kite. I'd better not be talking so big, I guess.

One of the boys lost his temper this morning and almost got eliminated. He was doing turns at 500 ft. That's not very high and you have to be careful. Anyway, the instructor gave him a good bawling out and said, 'so you like to go down, eh?' The instructor put the ship in a vertical dive at 500 ft. What does this kid do but push the throttle open and they were barely able to pull out in time. It scared the instructor silly and he was weak for quite a while after he landed. He couldn't say a whole lot because he started the whole thing. Well, there's not a lot more to say, so I'll close for now.

Your son, Lloyd

    Langdon receives more training, and confidence and is assigned to fly the famous Republic P-47.

Dale Mabry Field, Tallahassee, Florida - August 26, 1943

It seems quite a long time since I've written and still no answer. Something wrong?

You probably know that I'm now a hot Thunderbolt Driver. Lots of fun. They still keep us pretty busy. I can't say much, but please write.

Love, Lloyd

During the last few months of 1943, Langdon was assigned to the Eighth Air Force, 56th Fighter Group, 63rd Fighter Squadron based in Horsham, England. Langdon loved the P-47. He was proud to be flying with combat aces in one of the most famous fighter groups in the USAAF. The unit has been referred to as the "fighter group of aces."

England - January 31, 1944

Dear Dad,

This will be a crazy letter but right now I'm a little crazy. Yesterday, I made my fifth mission over enemy territory. Remember what you said when I was last home. To wit:
"Go in fighting and knock hell out of them." I haven't forgotten, Dad. Yesterday, I got at least two and maybe a third. It was a damn good feeling to pay Uncle Sam back for all my training in about 1 minute. If I never get another, I won't have been a losing investment.

I'll tell you what I can about it. My element leader and I were by ourselves and saw 15 enemy planes below getting ready to attack some B-24's. They were busy as hell trying to get into position and we slipped into them and knocked out 7 between us before they knew what hit them. Hall got two and damaged two and I got two and shot hell out of another before he broke away. My first caught fire and the second bailed out, so those are definite. I can only claim a

damaged on the third as I didn't see him catch fire or anything. "just a few hits on him."

I'm rather worried about how mom will take this. The thought of killing anyone like that is not a beautiful thought. He is human, but for myself, I feel just like I used to when I got a few rabbits in the old days. I feel very impersonal about the whole thing.

So much for now, Dad. I hope everyone's okay. I certainly am.

Write.

The above letter was the last letter Langdon wrote home. Three days later, February 3, 1944, Langdon ran out of gas on the return from a mission over Wilhelmshaven, Germany, and crashed into the North Sea. He was never heard from again. It was two weeks before the Langdon family received news that their son was missing. Langdon's mother, father and his eight siblings were devastated. Major Johnson, Commanding Officer HQ, 63rd Fighter Squadron sent the following account of Langdon's last flight to his parents.

All of the officers and men of this Squadron were greatly distressed when Lloyd did not return with the group on a recent mission. Knowing that you would desire to have all the facts pertaining to the mission, I am writing to give you such information as I have. On February 3, Lloyd was flying as the number two man in the red flight of our Squadron, as target

support to the bombers on a ramrod to Wilhelmshaven, Germany. Our Squadron had had several combats and was heading toward home when the supercharger regulator went out on the airplane of Captain Mahurin, the squadron leader. This forced him to drop below the top overcast of cloud to approximately ten thousand feet. Lt. Egan, red flight leader, took Lloyd, his wingman, with him and also dropped below the clouds to protect Captain Mahurin from any enemy aircraft that might be around. This was none too soon as when they broke through the clouds six Me 109's and two Fw190's started to attack Captain Mahurin and his wing man.

When the six Me 109's saw Lt. Egan and Lloyd coming in from above they rolled over and went straight down through the next lower overcast. The two Fw 190's, however, singled out Captain Mahurin's wingman and pressed home the attack. Lt. Egan and Lloyd were forced to fight for some time before gaining the advantage and forced the enemy aircraft to disengage and go down through the overcast. This prolonged, wide open engagement left them both very low on fuel, and approximately 200 miles from their home base.

Believing they could still make it, they headed toward the English coast on the shortest possible route. Approximately 40 miles from the English coast, off Felixstowe, Lloyd's plane ran out of gas and he was forced to go down. Lt. Egan circled above giving his position in order that Air Sea Rescue might be immediately instigated to pick Lloyd up if he had been able to bail out.

After all possible aid was given over the radio, Lt. Egan was forced to go on, and while still over water his plane also ran out of fuel. He was just able to glide to shore and make a crash landing on the beach. Lt. Egan had not been able to see Lloyd bail out, or his plane hit the water, before he ran out of gas. The Air Sea Rescue went to Lloyd's location immediately, but, due to the very high wind and rough sea, were not able to find any trace of a dinghy or the plane.

Lloyd was on his eighth operation flight. On the 30th of January, on a bomber escort mission to Brunswick, Lloyd destroyed two Me 109's and damaged another Me 109. These victories have been confirmed and copies of his personal combat report are enclosed.

Although Lloyd had only been in the Squadron a short time, he was most popular with everyone. His work was well done and he was always anxious to go on missions, always willing to do his share in our training program. Needless to say we will miss him a great deal. Our thoughts are with you during these days of distress.

My brother, Don, was eager to join the Marines and did so as soon as he graduated from high school not even waiting to get his diploma. Mom picked it up for him. Don was on the ship closest to the bombing of Hiroshima, Japan.

World War II ended in 1945 with the surrender of Germany on May 7, 1945 and Japan's surrender on August 15, 1945. The survivors would be coming home. The others were already home.

Lloyd's name is in the Roll of Honor Book in the American Memorial Chapel in St. Paul's Cathedral, London, England. This Memorial Chapel was dedicated in a service of commemoration of the American dead on July 4, 1951 with the Royal Family and General Dwight D. Eisenhower in attendance. It has been my privilege to have visited this beautiful memorial chapel in St. Paul's and have a staff member show me Lloyd's name listed in the Roll of Honor Book.

In January of 1953, the *LONDON TIMES* published a book entitled *BRITAIN'S HOMAGE TO 28,000 AMERICAN DEAD*. It is about the American Memorial in St. Paul's Cathedral and the Roll of Honor Book. Included in the Britain's Homage book is a message from Winston Churchill, who was Britain's Prime Minister during the war years. They sent a copy of the book to the folks with Lloyd's name imprinted on the front.

Lloyd's name is also on the Wall of the Missing at the Cambridge American Military Cemetery & Memorial, Coton, Cambridgeshire, England where there are services every Memorial Day which include the firing of volleys, taps and a fly-by. Don's daughter, Janice, attended this service in 1993 and recorded it for those of us back home.

The inscription on the Chapel Ceiling there is as follows:

"IN PROUD AND GRATEFUL MEMORY OF THOSE MEN OF THE UNITED STATES ARMY AIR FORCE WHO FROM THESE FRIENDLY

ISLES FLEW THEIR FINAL FLIGHT AND MET THEIR GOD. THEY KNEW NOT THE HOUR, THE DAY, NOR THE MANNER OF THEIR PASSING. WHEN FAR FROM HOME THEY WERE CALLED TO JOIN THAT HEROIC BAND OF AIRMEN WHO HAD GONE BEFORE. MAY THEY REST IN PEACE."

LLOYD AND HIS THUNDERBOLT - THE FIGHTIN' FILLY

Chapter 23

Lest we forget: Some last letters home

When the United Stated committed itself to war in 1941, the lack of war ships, aircraft, tanks, guns and other necessities for conducting a war on two oceans was frightening. Americans had to wind up to top speed in transforming her industrial skills overnight.

Our military was engaged in "fights-to-the-death" in the air, on the ground and on the seas. America's aircraft faced superior Japanese and German fighters in the skis over the Pacific islands and over Europe. The outcome of a victory or defeat could easily depend upon America's machinery of war. It was critical.

Not only did the United States gear-up for production, she also geared-up all ages of Americans who worked in the war plants. Many methods were used to inspire patriotism, duty, and hard work to set unprecedented production records.

Posters, movies, stories and pamphlets were created. War heroes, and movie stars, were invited to speak to production workers. As I was rummaging through some old WWII memorabilia, I came upon a small booklet which had been distributed to war production workers in WWII.

The booklet doesn't quite expand to the dimensions of a 5 by 7 inch booklet. It consists of eight pages, and is on thick paper yellowed by age. It has two staples holding it together. The staples are covered by a crust of rust, which has left its marks on the folds of the paper.

It was published by the Industrial Incentive Division, Navy Department, Washington, D. C. and printed by the

U. S. Government Printing Office in 1943. Glued onto the inside of the front cover is the following note:

```
YOUR ATTENTION PLEASE

DUE TO THE LIMITED SUPPLY, THE
NAVY REQUEST THAT YOU PASS
THIS BOOKLET ON TO YOUR
RELATIVES & FIRNEDS.

IT CONTAINS MANY INSPIRING,
HEROIC TALES FO THE FINE KIND
OF MEN WHO ARE GIVING THEIR ALL
FOR THEIR COUNTRY.
```

The print on the note is purple, designating it from the days of the old mimeograph machine. This booklet contains four letters written by navy men who never returned home, one letter from a survivor, and two presentations to war production factories; which are included in this chapter.

"My luck can't last much longer."

Below is an excerpt from a letter Ensign William R. Evans, Jr. wrote to a friend. Shortly after, Evans never returned from a flight with Torpedo Squadron 8 during the Battle of Midway on June 4, 1942.

"Many of my friends are now dead. To a man each died with a nonchalance that each would have denied courage, but simply called a lack of fear and forgot the triumph."

"If anything good or great has been born of this war, it should not be valued in the colonies we may win, nor in the pages that historians will attempt to write, but rather in the youth of our country who were never trained for war, and who almost never believed in war, but who have, from some hidden source, brought forth a gallantry which is homespun, it is so real."

"I say these things to you because I know you liked and understood boys, and because I want you to know that they have not let you down. Out here, between the spaceless sea and sky, American youth has found itself, and given of itself, so that a home spark may catch, burst into flame, and burn high. If our country takes these sacrifices with indifference, it will be the cruelest ingratitude the world has ever known."

"Remembering the countless happy hours I spent with all of you has been a constant source of contentment . . . My luck can't last much longer. But the flame goes on and only that is important."

"If I don't get back, you will have to be mother's protector."

Excerpt from the last letter Commander John J. Shea wrote to his five year old son, Jackie. Shea was reported missing after action aboard the USS Wasp on September 15, 1942.

"It is too bad that this war could not have been delayed a few more years so that I could grow up again with you and do all the things I planned to do when you were old enough to go to school....I miss you too, more than anyone will ever know. When you are a little bigger you will know why your daddy is not home so much any more."

"Fighting for the defense of our country, ideals, and homes is an honor and a duty which your daddy has to do before he can come home and settle down with you and mother. So wait a little longer."

"In the meantime, take care of your Mother and grow up to be a good young man. Study hard when you go to school. Be a leader in everything good in life. Play fair always. Be a good Catholic and you can't help being a good American."

"If I don't get back, you will have to be Mother's protector because you will be the only one she has. You must grow up to take my place as well as your own in her life and heart."

"Last of all, don't ever forget your Daddy. Pray for him to come back and, if it is God's will that he does not, be the kind of boy and man your Daddy wants you to be."

"At dawn tomorrow we are going in!"

Excerpt from a letter written by Henry Glorch, machinist mate first class, on the eve of the American invasion of the Solomon Islands. He was reported missing on August 8, 1942.

"This is one letter I hope you never get. Funny way to start a letter, isn't it? But it's the best I can do under the circumstances, because if you don't get it, that will mean I was very unfortunate."

"Tomorrow I will have the honor to participate in Uncle Sam's first move of retaliation against the Japs. And believe me, I can't wait. We have been preparing for this for a long time and now the time has come the to quit practicing and start doing."

"At dawn tomorrow we are going in and land United States Marines by the carload on the Japanese-held Islands."

"Our job, of course, is to get them to the beach as fast as we can. And we'll do it if we have to swim ashore with the marines on our back. Because I don't think in history a bunch of men have gone into any engagement as cool and calm and confident as this group. There is only one answer. It will be a success.

"As I write this I want you to know that I am not writing because I have any premonition of anything happening. I'm just writing because in case I do get mine, you'll know I got it like a man, and I am not afraid to die for my country."

"Believe that and please don't grieve, for this will all soon be over. I have only one regret and that is I could not see you once more. I loved my mother and father and family more than I ever said."

"All the boys I saw were carrying on like men!"

Excerpt from one of the last letters to his wife written by Rear Admiral Norman Scott, killed in action off Guadalcanal on the night of November 13th, 1942. Admiral Scott was posthumously awarded the Congressional Medal of Honor.

"Not so long ago I visited a hospital ship where a number of our wounded bluejackets and marines were being cared for. The ship was anchored in a port a long way from home."

"These words are intended as a tribute to the wounded I visited and for the information of the families with men in the Navy. I know that some of them are considered boys by their families, but all those I saw were carrying on like men."

"It has never been my privilege to have been received in the Navy or any place else, for that matter with such quiet friendliness and courtesy. Even those who were at the moment in pain would grind out 'I'll be all right!'"

"Not once during the entire visit was I answered with a grumble or a bellyache or a whine, but invariably with a grin or at least an attempt at one. Sometimes the answer would be low, and I would lean well over to make the conversation easier going. It might take a few seconds, and then I would hear 'I'm going pretty well, thank you, sir.' One like that and your heart goes right out to him."

"It is a custom in the Navy to remove one's cap in the sick bay. Mine will always be off to those men."

"In the deafening den, I remembered the men on Wake Island."

Excerpt from Marine Corps Private Albert Schmid's account of action at Guadalcanal. Credited with killing over 200 Japs, Schmid was awarded the Navy Cross for his part in this battle in which he was blinded.

"Our machine gun was positioned on the river bank where the stream was only 50 yards wide. Suddenly a huge bobbing mass scurried into the river. The Japs were starting to cross. 'No you don't, not tonight,' I whispered."

"Johnny Rivers swept our gun to and fro and the wading Japs crumbled. Except for some antitank fire upstream, we were the only opposition in our sector. Then Johnny got it in the face and I grabbed the gun."

"In the almost deafening din, I remembered the men on Wake Island. I swept my fire evenly across group after group of crack Jap troops. Lee Diamond was loading furiously when they got him. He fell across my legs. So I alternately loaded and fired. The gun got blistering hot in my hands. It made cracking and spitting noises. But it kept working right up to the end."

"I had just mowed down a particularly big party when all hell broke loose in our hole. Something struck me in the face. My helmet was knocked off. Everything became dark. I put my hands to my face and eyes. I felt blood and raw flesh."

"While we lay there, the Japs in the trees fired a steady downpour of bullets. It seemed my head would split open from pain. I strained my eyes, but I couldn't see. I worked around trying to get my .45 in my hand."

"Diamond kept saying, 'Keep down! Keep down!' "I said, 'The first Jap that jumps in here will be on the receiving end of this.'

" 'But you can't see!' "

" 'Yell which way he comes-I'll try to get him!'

"Some of these pilots who didn't come back could have come back!"

Excerpt from a description of the Battle of Midway, as told by Lieutenant Robert Lamb at an American war plant. Lamb was awarded the Navy Cross for extraordinary heroism.

"Our torpedo squadrons were the first of the naval striking forces to contact the enemy at Midway. This was our chance to pay the Japs back for Pearl Harbor and we didn't mean to miss."

"Three Jap Zero planes came at me as I dove towards their carrier. My gunner shot down one and the other two veered off. About 800 yards from the carrier and 50 feet over the water, I launched my torpedo. It seemed to be heading straight for the carrier. Then I got out of *there-fast.*"

"When I arrived at my carrier I found that only four out of fourteen planes in my squadron had returned safely. You people remember Midway as a great victory. I keep thinking of those ten pilots and ten gunners who didn't get back.

"Our squadron was flying old planes that day, planes that weren't nearly as fast or as well protected as our new machines. But when we returned to Pearl Harbor after the battle we found new planes for the whole squadron waiting for us on the field."

"That's what hurts. If someone had worked a little harder back home, if there hadn't been a delay somewhere along the line, we might have had those planes in time for the battle. And maybe-who can tell-maybe some of those ten pilots and ten gunners who *didn't* come *back-could* have come back."

"We weren't afraid of the planes, not that first time!"

Excerpt from a speech given at a war plant by Lt. Ann A. Bernatitus, only Navy Nurse to escape from the Philippines, and first person in the naval service to win the Legion of Merit award.

"Our hospital in Bataan was small, much too small for the number of wounded. Those who couldn't be bedded inside were put in cots in the open field. As many men were dying from sickness as from wounds. Bandages and gauze were so scarce that we washed out the old ones and used them again."

"That was the way matters stood the morning the Jap planes came over. We weren't afraid of the planes-not that first time. We had put huge red crosses to mark the hospital buildings and the fields."

"The Japs swept down very low. They couldn't have missed the crosses and they didn't miss the beds. Our men lay in the sun and waited for death from the sky."

"One terrible day we had 285 patients on our tables in 8 hours-a new patient every 2 minutes. One sailor was brought in with his abdomen blown to bits. 'Doctor,' he asked, 'is there any hope at all?' The doctor said reassuringly, 'We'll do everything we can.' The sailor tried to roll over. 'Doc,' he begged, 'get me off this table and save one of those other fellows who still has a fighting chance.'"

"Those men on Bataan deserve to be remembered. Not with flowers and memorials. It's too late for flowers and the monuments can wait. Remember them *now* by sending guns and planes and ships and tanks to other Americans wherever they're fighting. *That's* the way the men at Bataan would like to be remembered. Don't ever forget Bataan. Don't ever let it happen again to American fighting men any place in the world."

Photographs of Aircraft Mentioned In the Preceding Pages

Major Aircraft Represented In Chapters
(Heavy Bombers)

Consolidated B-24 Liberator

John McCullagh files

Boeing B-17 Flying Fortress

Photo by John McCullagh

Fighters

Republic P-47 Thunderbolt

North American P-51 Mustang

Photo by John McCullagh

Fighters

Vought F4U Corsair

www.vmf235.com

German Messerschmitt 109

http://en.wikipedia.org

Made in the USA
Las Vegas, NV
24 August 2021